A FRESH SEASON
Insights into Coaching, Leadership, and Volleyball

TERRY PETTIT

Additional copies may be purchased at www.terrypettit.com.
Published by Walsworth Publishing Co. Marceline, Missouri.
Cover photograph used with the permission of the University of Nebraska Athletic Department.

Many of these chapters were originally published in *Coaching Volleyball*, and other publications of the American Volleyball Coaches Association.

"Why I Don't Rate Players" first appeared in a book titled *Nebraska, the State of Volleyball*.

"The Top Ten Things I Wish I Had Known as a Freshman Collegiate Athlete," was written by Emma Pettit, Villanova volleyball, Class of 2016, and first appeared at *PrepVolleyball.com*.

.

ISBN: 978-1-4675-9300-7

A special thanks to Michelle Railsback Smith for editing, layout, and graphic design, and without whose help this book would still be on a "to do" list.

I would also like to thank the women that I had the opportunity to coach at the University of Nebraska and Louisburg College, who taught me how to coach, to my father, Harold Pettit, who taught me how to think, and to my wife, Anne, who makes it all work.

For the players I was
lucky enough to coach

CONTENTS

FOREWARD

Coach Pettit knows some of the best lessons in life come from a well-told story. When I played volleyball for him at the University of Nebraska he was my coach and mentor. Since then he has also become a peer and friend. I remember a lot about those days at Nebraska, but mostly I remember Coach's stories and the lessons behind them. Many of his former players would most likely agree. The moral of his stories not only applied to volleyball, but to the intricacies of life.

I loved playing for Coach. He taught me so much about volleyball and about the setting position. He's a master of Xs and Os and I loved talking volleyball with him. He understood the game in a way few coaches do. The most significant impact on my life were his lessons in leadership. Those lessons were key to my maturity as a player. He knows how to develop leaders better than just about anyone I've ever met. Of course, it wasn't always easy. Some days I could barely hold it together while Coach helped me find my ability to work through frustrations. He taught me resolve. John Maxwell says, "Believing in people before they have proven themselves is the key to motivating people to reach their potential." This is exactly what Coach was for me. I had my fair share of ups and downs during my college career, but through it all Coach believed in me, even when perhaps the facts told him otherwise. He saw in me a courage I didn't know I had and for that I will always be grateful.

Coach's competitiveness is something that people don't get to see as much these days. He was always competing. One day before practice he challenged me to a short court one-on-one game. I didn't doubt for a second that my twenty-year-old body would make quick work of my forty-something coach. Well, not only did I lose badly, but then had to listen to my teammates heckle me as I hung my head and walked back to the group. Apparently the lesson that day was on competing. Learning to embrace competition was something Coach always talked about, he engrained that in me. I never got another chance to play one-on-one with Coach, that was our one and only time, but I'd like to think if we played again today it would be a much closer game. It wouldn't be great volleyball. Neither one of us have quick twitch muscles left or a vertical jump to speak of, but I'm sure it would be competitive.

Since Coach Pettit retired from coaching, he's had a lot more time to write and tell stories, and that's the side of him I enjoy most. I remember our team meetings were often more story telling than pep talk. Coach would tell a story about one of his old teammates, or talk about the latest book he was reading, or the last movie he watched. If you paid attention, you would figure out how it related to you. His talks stayed with me, made me reflect. The same is true for the stories in this book. You don't need to be a volleyball coach or player to get something from these writings. Pay attention. A good story will always make you think and those are the stories that can change your life.

Christy Johnson-Lynch
Heach Volleyball Coach, Iowa State University &
Nebraska Volleyball Player, 1991-95

INTRODUCTION: INSTEAD OF A RESUMÉ

Sometimes I am asked if I would ever return to coaching. If I were interested in a position, this is what I would send:

Education:
B.S. in English, Manchester College 1968
M.F.A. in Creative Writing, the University of Arkansas 1974
3,467 hours in timeouts: 1974-2000

Previous Job Experience:
I have interviewed for jobs on the western shore of Maryland; Chapel Hill, North Carolina; Eugene, Oregon; the foothills of Tennessee and Virginia; and found one in eastern Nebraska at the edge of a salt marsh where I stayed for twenty-seven years.

Personal Tastes:
In cars, I like hybrids and old Porsche roadsters.
My favorite play is *Inherit the Wind*.
Borges and Chekhov would make good bookends in fiction.
I like dark chocolate before dinner and rhubarb pie for dessert.
The Buffalo River in north central Arkansas is the wildest stream I've ever floated. The night before the canoe trip we slept in the loft of an abandoned barn, our dreams, a conspiracy of anticipation.

Movies:
Deliverance is one of the few movies I've watched more than once.
The Last Tango in Paris made sense the second time, thirty years later.
The two most magical scenes in the cinema for me are when the catcher arrives in *Field of Dreams* and the last five minutes of *Cinema Paradiso*.

Additional Experience:
Wrigley Field is where I bought my first and only tethered chameleon. When I was three I fell out of the car and tumbled down a hill in Burbank, California, before my father retrieved me, pretty much unharmed except for a blackened front tooth.

Religious Affiliation:
I am part Presbyterian and part Brethren, minus the black hats and horses.
My favorite bird is the great blue heron, and whenever I see one, pulling darkness over the prairie, I think we are going to win.
The first brook trout I caught was on light spinning tackle and a barbless panther martin in Jeremy's Run near Luray, Virginia.
I love the sound of a North American river.
I believe in great horned owls and middle attackers flying in transition.

Political Bent:
I've marched once to end a war: down Michigan Avenue in 1968 with other students, ministers, musicians, and conscientious objectors, all of us powerless beyond our choice of shoes.
I believe our national anthem should be *City of New Orleans*, Arlo or Willie, take your pick.
I like coyotes, blues, and people who don't ask for a menu. The bicycle is my favorite invention.
The most effective serve is to pin a receiver on her left hip near the left sideline.

Music:
On the road I listen to James Taylor, Van Morrison, Mellencamp, and jazz.

Coaching Philosophy:
I love timeouts. I love coaching against teams that may well beat us. I love the flare of nostrils before the big match. I love asking the players, the assistants, and myself to be uncomfortable in our preparation.

I am not committed to any one specific defense, tempo, or tactical decision. I am better at requiring than relating, but I'll make the effort.

Each team is an adventure. Nothing guaranteed; what I've come to understand is that the monkeys always come. The first requirement for coaching is hope. The second is a setter, foolish in her passion.

Miscellaneous:
The Fourth of July is my least favorite holiday, except for flying into the capital city at dusk once and seeing the shooting stars below, with rockets coming toward the plane like telephone poles.

Recreation and Entertainment:
I am not interested in a job unless there is a stream near town with fish that need cool running water. I love a golf course that has a short par-four requiring finesse, and a neighborhood diner that serves red beans and rice. *Recruiting quickness is my addiction.*

References:
I took a class in how to end a poem from the father of Lucinda Williams. Once, on a cold winter evening in Chicago, I heard Elizabeth Bishop read her poem, *The Fish*.
Twice I sat at the same table with Bob Gibson.

Warning to the Athletic Administration:
I am not good at small talk. At times I may seem distracted and aloof. I have a poor short-term memory; I need bifocals to read and fins to swim. I love to attack a weakness in the third rotation. If this is a good fit, please accept this application. I am eager to meet you. I will do my best.

A LETTER TO THE PARENTS OF A PROSPECTIVE RECRUIT

I would like to see college coaches educate the parents of their recruits with the following message and commitment:

When your daughter comes to "State University," I pledge that we will use all our resources to give her the opportunity to develop into an outstanding volleyball player, student, and citizen. We will not physically or mentally abuse her. We will not run her off to another school when we have the opportunity to recruit someone with more talent. We will treat her the same way we would like our own child to be treated, which means there will be times when she will be challenged, encouraged, and pushed to do things beyond what she believes she is capable. This is my commitment to you.

Here is the commitment I need from you, the parents:

There will be times in your daughter's collegiate career where she may be frustrated, anxious, or angry for any of the following reasons: She may find the expectations more than she anticipated. She may be asked to play a role on the team that is not the one she dreamed of. She may not enjoy competing every day against other athletes as skilled and talented as she is. She may not yet have an appreciation for delayed gratification. She may interpret information as judgment. She may long for something else that appears easier or more comfortable. She may be overwhelmed by a combination of these factors.

If she is, then she is having a normal college experience which is typical for someone who is moving through adolescence to adulthood. When this happens, there will come a moment when she calls or texts you and wants to do one of the following: leave school and come home, transfer to another school, or organize a plot to get me fired.

I need you to make the commitment that when your daughter calls you will listen, you will communicate your love for her, and then you will tell her to get back to the tough business of growing up and becoming accountable for the challenges she is lucky enough to have before her. If you cannot make this commitment then you need to look at other schools. If you can, fasten your seatbelt and welcome aboard.

COACHING THE COACH
IN THE MIRROR

The three benchmarks many coaches look for when evaluating a recruit are: talent, attitude, and effort. To that I would add a fourth: the willingness of an athlete to be uncomfortable as she develops. This combination usually leads to an exceptional player.

As coaches we don't think of ourselves as performers; we consider ourselves teachers and leaders, and yet I believe that holding ourselves to the same standards we use to evaluate a player is a reasonable way to measure our preparation and work habits.

It is a cliché to say coaches work hard, but there is at least as much variance in how hard and focused individual coaches work as there is between athletes in their commitment and preparation to reach a goal. There are head coaches who are working fifteen hours a day to make a program better and there are coaches checking in at 10:00 a.m. and punching out after practice. While there are some successful coaches who can err on the side of thinking too much about their program (I can think of one head coach who cannot sit through an entire movie without thinking about how to make her third rotation stronger), I know of very few consistently successful high school and college coaches who are not out-working their competition.

Are there programs that begin with significant advantages? Yes. It is *easier to interest* a recruit in Stanford, Texas, or Florida than it is to some of their competitors. But even at those schools, sustained success is not as easy as it would appear. If Stanford were to put together two or three consecutive seasons where they did not compete for a conference championship it would dramatically impact their recruiting. Recruiting is very fickle. It is not always where you are ranked that is important but the direction that public opinion believes you are moving. Two recruiting mistakes in the same year combined with an injury can send a program spiraling to a different level.

We all know how important a positive attitude is for the people we are coaching, and each of us could list at least a couple of players who never reached their potential because of their sense of entitlement or the fact that they just didn't get it. The same can be true of coaches. There are assistant coaches who believe they are not getting the opportunity to become head coaches because of their gender, when in fact, it is their decision to see themselves as victims that prevents their development.

There are head coaches who take far fewer risks than they ask of their athletes. In scheduling, networking, and recruiting they choose to play it safe. Why go after the better players when I am more likely to be rejected? Why schedule stronger competition when we are more likely to be defeated? Why network with peers when it is more comfortable to communicate with people I already have a relationship with? Why develop an offense different from other teams when if it doesn't work I will look foolish? Why work at increasing our attendance when we have so much competition from professional sports? Why continue to work at building something remarkable when the person I report to is only interested in us being competitive?

Many of us could not respond to the same demands and expectations we place on our student-athletes if an administrator placed similar demands on us. We ask athletes to be uncomfortable every day. We ask them to set goals and to lay a foundation through strength training, nutrition, and conditioning that will give them the best chance to reach their target. We ask them to stay in town during the summer so that they can develop a sense of purpose with their teammates, and we ask them to work camps so they can understand the game from a different perspective. We ask them to refine fundamentals, and if we are great coaches, we never stop asking.

What do we ask of ourselves? How uncomfortable are we willing to be? Do we travel each year to spend a couple of weeks learning from our peers? Do we spend a month during the spring visiting a junior program within our region? Do we develop local and regional coaches? Do we develop relationships with better coaches that will impact our scheduling? Do we watch men's volleyball and try to determine what aspects of the men's game we could apply to our own? Do we hire assistant coaches with talents better than our own or do we choose comfort over talent? Who do we ask to help us to hold ourselves accountable?

Talent, effort, attitude, and the willingness to be uncomfortable are characteristics that are just as important in coaching as they are in a prospective team captain. So consider strapping this compass to your wrist: Did I work as hard today as my middle blocker? Did I take more risks than the freshman to whom I am teaching new footwork? Am I as open minded to new ideas and fundamentals as the setter I am trying to retrain? Do I reflect the passion I want from our libero? Am I projecting an attitude that the culture we are building is getting better every day, or am I caught up in a cycle of defeatism and victim-hood? We all know the athlete who spends more energy trying not to work hard than it would take to embrace the opportunity. Sometimes we can be that person.

TERRY PETTIT

WHY I DON'T RATE PLAYERS

John Cook, my friend and head volleyball coach at the University of Nebraska, contacted me recently and asked me if I would list the top two players at each position (two complete teams of six) who had ever played volleyball for Nebraska. He was asking on behalf of two people at the *Lincoln Journal Star* who are writing a book on the history of Nebraska volleyball.

I politely declined for a couple of reasons. First of all, one of my purposes as a head coach was to find a way for each individual player to reach her potential. My focus was not so much on whether or not they were better than their teammate or teammates from previous teams, but whether or not they were continuing to develop and take on new challenges as they moved through their college careers.

Secondly, it is impossible for me to compare players who competed in different years, let alone different decades. Collegiate volleyball in 2013 is neither easier nor harder than it was in previous decades, but it *is* different. Terri Kanouse (1978-81), Karen Dahlgren (1983-87), Virginia Stahr (1986-89), Stephanie Thater (1989-92), Allison Weston (1992-95), Megan Korver (1996-98), and Amber Holmquist (1999-2001) were among the NCAA All-American middle blockers that I had the good fortune to coach.

All but Holmquist played when there was no libero and were primary passers and back row defenders, as well as strong net players. Dahlgren, the 1986 Broderick Award Winner, was the first Nebraska player (and perhaps the first collegiate player) to run the slide. It was like coming onto the court with a machine gun when the opponent had a bow and a quiver of arrows.

Jenny Kropp (1999-2001) played perhaps as strong a match as any Husker has ever played in the NCAA Division I Final Four when Nebraska beat Hawaii, 3-1, in the 2000 semifinals. Korver was a key player on a team that returned to the Final Four with only two returning starters. She also had the final kill in transition in what some people consider the best Husker home match of all time, when Nebraska beat Penn State in the 1996 NCAA Regionals, 20-18, in the fifth game.

Weston, the 1995 NCAA Player of the Year, was the best transition middle attacker in the country her junior and senior seasons, but was strong enough in her all-around skills to be a team captain as an outside hitter on the 2000 U.S. Olympic Team.

Kanouse, a three-time Big Eight Conference MVP and Nebraska's first All-American, played before the development of the slide ,which would have made her an even stronger player because of her explosiveness off the floor.

Stahr was a three-time All-American who played in two national championship matches, one of them as a senior following shoulder surgery.

Holmquist was the strongest blocker in the country her final two seasons, but saw fewer sets because of an offense that was oriented to outside hitters. Had she played on a team that focused on her strengths she might have been as dominant offensively.

I didn't have the opportunity to coach Melissa Elmer (2002-05) or any of the other exceptional Husker middle blockers of the past decade so it would be impossible for me to have a clear perspective on their talents.

Each of the players that I have mentioned had the opportunity to play for an extraordinary setter. Mary Buysee (1981-84), Cathy Noth (1981-84), Tisha Delaney (1985-86), Lori Endicott (1985-88), Val Novak (1987-90), Nikki Stricker (1990-93), Christy Johnson (1991-95), Fiona Nepo (1995-98), Grecialy Cepero (1999-2001), Rachel Holloway (2005-07), Sydney Anderson (2008-10), and Lauren Cook (2010-12) were among the top setters in the country and each of them had their own unique talents. When those talents complimented the middle attackers on their team, something magical could happen.

Nebraska has an equally strong history at the outside hitter and right side positions, and I'm sure it is fun for fans or journalists to make lists of their hypothetical top six. But for someone who has coached such talented and competitive people, I cannot tell you, in all honesty, which players would win starting positions if all of Nebraska's great players played at the same time.

The real thing to celebrate about Nebraska volleyball is not which players won the most awards or hit or blocked for the highest percentage, but a culture and community that encourages talented women to be willing to risk everything in their individual journeys so that a team can be better. Watching Laura Pilakowski (1999-2002) motivated Jordan Larson's (2005-08) development. Endicott came to Nebraska because of Noth, and followed her to the U.S. National Team. Johnson's leadership emerged from competing on a daily basis with Stricker.

This is what players know, that fans can only sense, when a team accomplishes something extraordinary. Championships only happen when everyone is doing everything possible to reach the goal. Dahlgren does not lead the country in attack percentage if Delaney is not setting her and Enid Schonewise (1983-86) and Kathi DeBoer (1984-87) are not exceptional passers.

Weston is not the national player of the year if Johnson does not have the courage to set Billy Winsett (1992-95) and Kate Crnich (1993-96), who combine for fifty kills in a national championship match which depends on a reserve freshman setter, Nepo, coming off the bench to serve an ace at a critical moment in the final game.

So for me, asking which Huskers are better than others is like ranking the legs, tail, and heart of a leopard in pursuit. There are no most valuable parts . . . it just arrives.

TERRY PETTIT

GROWING UP IN THE GOLDEN
RECTANGLE OF BACKYARD BALL

Our backyard was 120 feet by seventy feet; a golden rectangle of sorts before I knew such a concept existed. To the east, down the third base line, was a chain link fence behind which was an abandoned orchard of apple, pear, and plum trees. To the north and south were the Rettigs and Reids, whose families produced six kids, two girls in the former and four boys in the later, all of them between Little League age and high school. To the west was our home, a 1,200 square-foot ranch, with three bedrooms trimmed with small rectangular windows that were so narrow we could barely sneak out of them during the dog days of summer when we were supposed to be taking a nap.

This is where our mother cooked, kept house, and laid out our clothes; and where our father returned in the early afternoon from delivering milk to play catch. It was also where my two brothers and I reluctantly slept when we were called in from the backyard or somewhere down the neighborhood, which earned the nickname "the fertile valley" because of the seventy or so kids that floated in and out of homes with open windows.

The featured attraction in the backyard was a clay basketball court built by our father as a Christmas gift when I was in sixth grade. It was popular because, unlike the other courts in the neighborhood that relied on backboards affixed to a garage where the court fell away to the street at an angle, our court was level and so you didn't have to make the Pythagorean adjustment to your shot as you moved away from the goal.

(We had another court inside our bedroom where a New Era potato chip can served as a basket for tennis balls or wadded up socks and where the drywall had to be replaced twice because of enthusiastic play.)

Behind the clay court was a twenty-foot screen, our own green monster that my father installed when Mr. Rettig returned home and discovered the image of a Wilson Indestructo basketball on the siding of his new garage. A Schlitz-inspired phone call to my father led to a heated conversation that resulted in three telephone poles with 200 square feet of chicken wire protecting the garage from future Indestructo attacks. (I am not making the Indestructo name up. Wilson also made Indestructo footballs, golf bags, and for all I know, Indestructo jock straps and baseball cups.)

The court did my brother Jack much more good than me. I was cut from the high school basketball team my junior year while Jack was an all-conference player for two years and earned a combined baseball-basketball scholarship to Valparaiso University. My only lasting impression from the court is a scar on my left leg which resulted from being pushed into a bush by my father as I attempted a left-handed hook shot in a competitive game of one-on-one. The shrub was fifteen feet to the left of the goal and had been planted there to keep errant passes from running down to the corner of the lot where home plate sat for multiple baseball-type games.

Forty-six feet from home plate was a pitching mound situated diagonally across the yard at the official Little League distance. Jack and I took turns pitching to each other from the mound or pitching to a life-size screen my father had built that consisted of a six-foot high rectangle with inner tubes stretched and woven across the frame. A rectangular strike zone was painted onto the inner tubes with a right-handed batter crowding the plate. A few years later a sporting goods company developed a much smaller aluminum version of this set up called a "pitch back" that can still be purchased today.

In the southeast corner of the yard a coffee can was sunk into the lawn with a makeshift flag we could chip to with seven irons. We trimmed the grass around the cup with hand clippers to make it look like a putting green. Twenty feet to the east was a pole vault pit that I built with standards made from leftover lumber from a house being built on the other side of the neighborhood, although the contractor didn't see it that way.

The pole vault pit was sawdust and discarded foam pillows, while both the pole vault pole and the crossbar were "genuine" bamboo. Heights of more than six feet were achieved but that was the limit, because if you approached the pit with any more speed you would not only vault over the bar but onto the wire fence that separated our yard from the Reids next door.

The Reid's yard was significant because if you hit a home run with a Wiffle ball, mush ball, or a deflated basketball if the first two weren't available, it required you to knock the ball over our house or over the left field fence into the Reid's yard. There was only one kid in the neighborhood who could take any kind of ball over the house. Our parents' only intervention was to declare that anything hitting the house was an automatic out and so everyone but Jim Knight became a pull hitter.

The games were frequently co-ed. The Rettig girls, Patty and Barbara, continued to play even after the confrontation between their father and our father. No harm, no foul. As all of us moved toward adolescence there was one concession to gender. In mush ball games the boys had to swing the bat with one hand while the Rettigs could swing with two. Patty was thin and primarily a singles hitter; but Barbara Rettig had a large frame, and as I remember there was some discussion as she moved through puberty about having her swing with one hand as well when she began to belt mush balls into the Reid's backyard with alarming consistency.

We played football in the yard as well, although you wouldn't recognize it as such. One player would hike the ball to himself and everyone else would tackle him. You had four downs to get from one fence line to the other. No one ever got hurt, partly because speed was never a factor; if there were four or more players, the person with the ball was tackled before they could take two steps. Looking back on this, it was not much different than young goats butting each other.

Wiffle ball was the game of the last common denominator because you only needed two people to play it. We threw in-shoots, out-shoots, rise balls, and drop balls, and if you had a big lead and wanted to taunt the batter, you could throw an off-speed pitch which could easily result in a home run. But if you got a whiff from your brother you could also bring about pre-pubescent *schadenfreude*, the closest thing to pure joy for a sixth grader. While mush ball disappeared with high school, Wiffle ball continued throughout high school until the neighborhood kids went off to college or jobs in the steel mills to the north in Gary, Indiana.

There were games that didn't work out as well in the backyard. Several winters we tried to flood the basketball court and convert it into an ice rink with only marginal success, certainly nothing like the fun we had skating at Bowman's pond or the backwash of the Kankakee River. One fall we cut young willows from a ditch on a county road and put up a teepee on the basketball court by stretching tarpaper (there was still construction in the neighborhood), but it had to come down when we wanted to play "horse" or "around the world."

Things started to go in a different direction with the summer of the carnival. The idea was to create a midway in the backyard and charge a modest amount, a nickel for each attraction or twenty-five cents for an all day pass, to younger neighborhood kids who might not know better. First we made several trips to the furniture store downtown and got as many refrigerator and washing machine boxes as we could. Then Jack and I spent the morning cutting and taping cardboard boxes, creating a midway of animal acts, amusements, mind reading, and concessions.

Because there were only two of us, Jack had to climb out from under the box when someone wanted to see a different attraction. I would collect the money while Jack was hidden in the cardboard box. Our dog, one of several we named Buster, didn't look much like a tiger but he was not all that dissimilar from one of those disappearing carnivores in Australia, and he was willing to stay in a wagon with a box on top.

We had a candy machine that dispensed lemon drops for a penny. You could win baseball cards, but no Chicago Cubs or St. Louis Cardinals, if you sank a shot behind the free throw line for a nickel. You could have your fortune written out on a small piece of paper as long as one of us said your name loud enough so the other brother could hear it beneath a card table tent. We had magic tricks that worked if you were under ten, but mostly we just had a lot of decorated cardboard that didn't do much.

Toward the end of the day a photographer showed up. We were horrified because our mom was so impressed with what we were doing she had called the *Lake County Register*, a weekly paper, and a teenage photographer who lived nearby came over with his 35-millimeter camera. I think he thought our carnival was an attempt to con loose change from little kids because he took one look at the scattered boxes and our clientele, snapped a photograph, and departed on his Huffy.

The receipts from the carnival left us with less than two dollars and a yard full of trash to haul away. But one of us came up with a great idea; an idea even better than the carnival itself. We gathered the remaining neighborhood kids around us and made them an offer: "Who would like to buy an entire circus, minus a rare Australian Tasmanian Devil, for a quarter?" The Reid brothers stepped up; and to show our appreciation we didn't even accept the twenty-five cents but just asked for their help in throwing the remnants of the midway over the left field fence into their yard. The only thing that would have made it better would have been if the Rettig sisters had a younger brother so we could have dumped the stuff up against their garage behind the chicken wire screen.

TERRY PETTIT

THE PROBABILITY OF A GIRAFFE WEARING A TRENCH COAT

On January 15, 2009, when Captain C.B. "Sully" Sullenberger realized that U.S. Airways Flight 1549 was losing power after hitting a flock of geese soon after taking off from LaGuardia Airport, his first decision was to announce to the cockpit he was taking control of the plane. Was there any way of predicting when Sullenberger first became a pilot forty years before, that he would develop the expertise, leadership, and command under pressure which would allow him to land an airbus in the Hudson River without loss of life?

Every day the brightest minds make mistakes in probability. There are sure-bet baseball phenoms that never blouse their pants in the major leagues, while the leading candidates for the Republican presidential nomination flame out as distant "also-rans" less than a year later. Is it possible to tell whether or not someone who is a very good assistant coach is going to be an extraordinary head coach? Is it possible to tell whether someone who was a great player can build a solid high school program? Will someone who thrives as a coach in Wyoming excel in Louisiana?

Could anyone have predicted Christy Johnson's startling success at Iowa State when she was an assistant coach at Wisconsin? Was there anything in Teri Clemens' biography in 1985 to suggest she was on the cusp of a career that would lead Washington University (St. Louis) to seven national championships, including six consecutive? Who thought a hospital corpsman in the U.S. Navy named Chuck Erbe, would revolutionize how volleyball players are trained in the mid-70s?

Coaching trees are not a reliable predictor of coaching success. There are coaches who have won national championships who can point to less than two or three former players and assistants who have become successful head coaches. Until recently, even a coach as revered as Duke's Mike Krzyzewski could not claim a single extraordinary protégé. Talent beats coaching tree.

So the question becomes, are there *any* predictors to hiring a head coach? I think there are, but I'll forewarn you the following is based on my own observations, not on scientific research:

1.   I believe having previous success as a head coach is a predictor similar to the relationship of high school grades and the potential for a college degree. It takes talent and vision to win consistently in any arena. Thank God there is no ACT or SAT for coaching. It would tell us nothing about motivation, will, or persistence. All things being equal (and they frequently are not), I would give the nod to someone who has worn the mantle of a successful head coach, whether it is junior ball, college coaching, or the Minden Whippets.

2.   There is no commitment without passion. A prospective coach doesn't have to arrive for the interview on a pogo stick, but he can't come across as if coaching is just one of his options. You almost have to have the feeling the candidate lives to coach. Life would be unbearable if he couldn't say, "corner up" at least once a day. It was Einstein who implied: *coaching = energy squared.*

3.   Integrity is not an option. Everybody makes mistakes. People with integrity do not keep making the same mistake. Does the candidate have a history of undermining head coaches? Does the coach operate from a position of what he can get away with, or does he do what's right, even when it may make his team less competitive?

4.   Does he complain about what he doesn't have, or does he find a way to get things done even without the administrative support he would like to have? Does he see himself as a victim or a leader?

5.   Is he evolving and reinventing himself with his understanding of the game, or is he stuck in the trappings of style and outdated teaching? Is he willing to learn something from his peers or has intellectual laziness become a brand?

6.   Will he embrace the culture of the school and the community? Are his values and goals consistent with the administration who hires him?

7.   Is he curious? Does he read everything he can about competition and leadership? Does he travel to Japan or to the next county to explore a different way of training a setter? Is he willing to adapt and innovate, or has his brain become a comfortable hammock?

8.   Can he walk the difficult line of requiring and caring? Can he set his ego aside and recognize the needs of a player without letting go of what she can become? Can he collaborate or is he so insecure that leadership and coaching become more style than substance: a giraffe wearing a trench coat?

9.   Does he have a sense of humor? Humor not only indicates a path to the right side of the brain, but also makes him more bearable to be around when he pulls the fire alarm because the libero forgot to cover.

10.   Is it about the purpose of the program, or is it about him? Both types of coaches can win, but only one requires you to wash your hands each time your greet him.

I cannot tell you which of these is most important. But with extraordinary coaches these and other values are integrated in such a way that you know you are in the presence of an adult. That does not mean they know all there is to know about their sport, but rather that they know who they are and what values they will not compromise. They are verbs, not modifiers, and when they walk onto the court everybody wants to join them in going to work.

TERRY PETTIT

HOW CAN WE JUSTIFY
INTERCOLLEGIATE ATHLETICS?

I believe the purpose of a university education is to teach people to learn how to learn, and to learn how to take responsibility for their own development. There are other things which take place of course: the memorization of scientific tables, learning how to write a readable essay, the reading of great and not so great literature, the socialization that comes with living in dormitories, fraternities, and sororities, and the introduction of the arts and music through required attendance at recitals and exhibitions. But all of this to me is secondary to the idea that a college education is one way we can learn various approaches of taking accountability for our own development.

For the sake of the argument, let's assume you agree with me. If so, *what is the purpose of intercollegiate athletics?* How can we justify spending millions of dollars on a small percentage of the student population? Some might argue we can justify football and men's basketball because they provide entertainment for the university and local communities, and in some cases generate revenue which allows other students to participate in the competitive arena.

If revenue is the primary justification for an athletic department, universities would be better off taking the football budget and investing it in Berkshire Hathaway, Apple, or Google. If entertainment is the primary goal then we could take the money and have Cirque du Soleil troupes visit the campus quarterly and provide free tickets to every student, faculty member, administrator, and donor.

The best justification I can find for the amount of money we spend on intercollegiate athletics returns me to my original premise: *if a university education is where we go to learn how to learn, then an athletic department can be a laboratory for that endeavor.*

My vision is for coaches to have the potential to build a culture which promotes self-actualized leadership, one where student-athletes progress from being directed and coached, to becoming situational leaders who become passionate about their own development. The first step in the process is to give student-athletes a framework for making better decisions.

Here is a list of values a coach or athletic department might consider when developing a compass for decisions:

- Integrity
- A strong work ethic
- Teamwork
- Tolerance and respect for teammates, opponents, and others outside our community
- A willingness to be uncomfortable in the pursuit of excellence

The last value interests me in particular. Given the nature of contemporary culture where many incoming student-athletes have had even their smallest problems solved by their parents, we have to begin by changing the mindset that accompanies the people we are coaching. We have to educate both them and their parents that to do our job we will create a supportive environment which continually challenges student-athletes to take responsibility for themselves and their personal development.

Our first task is to teach our players how to make better decisions. Imagine if the values I listed above were like the directions on a compass, and we teach our athletes to hold each decision they make up to those values. (You could even make a wristband that each player wore listing the core values.)

At the end of a tough practice the head coach decides he will push the team through a series of shuttle runs to develop fitness and mental toughness. The player has a decision to make. Do I glide through the exercise, working hard enough to stay ahead of a few other players so as to not draw attention to myself; or do I push myself as hard as I can? Which decision is consistent with the values and behaviors my teammates and I have committed to uphold?

Is there *integrity* in giving less than my best effort? No.
Do I have *respect for my teammates* if I do not work hard? No.
Am I honoring my commitment to be *uncomfortable*? No.

It is more likely team members (and coaches) will hold themselves accountable to difficult tasks if they have already committed to specific behaviors before the challenge is in front of them.

Does this mean everyone wearing a wristband will automatically become a great teammate? No. Does it mean everyone will automatically give their best effort in every drill? No. But even when they do not choose the behavior consistent with our sense of purpose, they will be aware of it. Our first goal is awareness. Our next goal is not to be perfect, but to be better. What we are trying to do is move from *directing* a player into the appropriate behavior to *coaching* a player who has already committed to specific values and behaviors which give her the best chance to get better.

As coaches we tend to see our most difficult challenges in physical terms: blocking footwork, defensive pursuit, left side attack against a strong block in endgame, etc. . . . But every behavior we hope to create on the court is preceded by a decision in the brain. Leadership is making decisions based on predetermined values. We have to train leadership as consistently and as passionately as we do transition footwork or any other sophisticated response that leads to success. Leadership cannot develop until we first teach our team members how to follow a commitment to healthy values and behaviors.

TERRY PETTIT

TEACHING PRINCIPLES FOR JUNIOR VOLLEYBALL COACHES TO CONSIDER

- I believe the purpose of an education is to teach young people how to learn. Volleyball is a laboratory for learning how to learn. It is where we apply the best information we have while creating an environment for young athletes to accelerate the learning process.

- Fundamentals are at the heart of the learning process. The more fundamentally sound a player is, the more consistent she will be under pressure. The more fundamentally sound a player is, the more creative she can be.

- In developmental volleyball (fourteen and under) approximately two-thirds of the time spent in practice should be on very specific fundamental development. The other one-third can be spent in a variety of different ways: incorporating fundamentals into systems, competitive games which emphasize fundamental behaviors, and team drills that simulate situations that happen in live play.

- The Millennials (the kids we are coaching) are used to taking in information visually. They can have some difficulty when new information is given to them verbally. What this means is learning will take place faster when we demonstrate (model) drills and new concepts. Initially some drills may have to be modeled each time they are run until players take ownership of all of the movements, posture, and behaviors they are being asked to learn.

• In general, younger players cannot focus for more than ten to twelve minutes in a specific drill without the quality of the repetitions deteriorating.

• Millennials respond to structure. The more we use structure (goals and specific requirements), the higher the quality of learning that will take place.

• Coaches need to understand the difference between "style" and "fundamental." Whether or not a player bounces a ball as part of her serving routine is style; whether or not she strikes the ball when she is balanced on her front foot is fundamental.

• Players focus best when they are given a specific way to end a drill; the goal of this drill is to have fifteen successful repetitions. When we reach our goal the drill is over.

• Players should be given a "focus" even when they are warming up. For example if we are asking them to "warm-up" by serving the ball over the net, we should require they serve at a specific target and focus on a specific sequence and movement.

• As much as possible, coaches' communication with players during a drill should be done with "key words." The players will associate key words with specific behaviors, such as shift your "platform" to the target, "load" your hips on attack, and use a "butterfly" hand position when blocking.

• While developmental volleyball is about learning a baseline in all facets of the game, coaches should be alert to specific talents that can be leveraged with each player. The more time that can be spent in leveraging a player's specific talent, the greater the impact she will have on the team.

• It is particularly helpful in the learning process for coaches to educate players that information is not judgment. The younger the player, the more likely they are to interpret information as, "I'm doing something wrong." This is why we need to use "key" words, which are more likely to be heard as information rather than judgement.

• One of the most difficult evaluations a coach has to make when a player is *not* doing a specific behavior correctly is whether or not the undesirable result is because of a lack of effort, or a lack of execution? Effort is non-negotiable. Execution requires patience.

• If a practice is longer than two hours (including warm-up) then the coach has done a poor job in practice planning. It is difficult to have a college player's focus for two hours; and when we require more than that from developing juniors, we are running an inefficient practice and diluting the learning that is taking place.

• If a practice is run crisply there will not be a great deal of conditioning needed beyond the practice. If we do incorporate conditioning into practice it is best to do it with movements that replicate the behaviors we are trying to teach: spike approaches, blocking movements, run-thrus, etc. Conditioning is better at the end of practice because if it is done at the beginning, the resultant fatigue can impact the quality of learning that takes place.

• Learning takes place in a drill progression where there is little interference (the exception to this is when you are training players to work through or ignore interference). Asking a player to learn more than one concept at a time creates interference.

• Volleyball is a game where the team that makes the fewest errors wins. This is true at both the international level and in developmental volleyball. The simpler the side-out or transition system we use, the less potential we have for creating errors that are system-based.

• In developing systems the most important decisions we have to make are: What are our strengths, and how can we leverage them?

- Systems can be designed with the following considerations:

  1. Setting: The setter touches the ball more than twice as much as any other player. She has the opportunity to better the ball with every contact. Good setting and average hitting will defeat good hitting and average setting.

  2. Passing: Players will develop touch if they are asked to pass the ball with a specific arc that is no higher than the top of the antenna. If they are just required to pass the ball to a target without regard to the arc, they may not develop any feel.

  3. Attacking: In developmental volleyball less than one-third of the points will come from attack; two-thirds will come from errors. This concept should enter into the development of our systems (and should be trained into the mindset of our players).

- Maybe the most important concept in a coach's development is insight into the differences between talent and skill, and how each can be leveraged.

Example: Teaching someone to set a volleyball is primarily a skill. Teaching someone to get to the volleyball in a balanced position is primarily a talent.

There is a window that closes in the mid-teens where the optimum learning takes place. Arm speed, footwork, lateral movement, soft eyes, etc., are very difficult to teach if that learning does not take place before or during puberty. That is why sound fundamental training and concepts are so critical in the fourteen-and-under teams.

THE SEVEN IRREFUTABLE LAWS OF BEING AN ELEPHANT

There are books on coaching and leadership that provide as much hope for becoming a leader as "The Seven Irrefutable Laws of Being an Elephant" give hope to a dingo longing to become a pachyderm:

1. With captive exceptions, you have a better chance of being an "authentic" elephant if you were born in Thailand, India, or Africa.

2. Take a look in the mirror. Do you appear to be larger than a truckload of refrigerators?

3. When you put a nickel in the scale at the amusement park, does your fortune read, "Come back when you're by yourself."?

4. Do you have a strong sense of family and enjoy rubbing up against each other even when one of you is dead?

5. Do you enjoy displacing and spraying large amounts of brackish water on yourself?

6. Does everyone in the animal kingdom (cheetahs, enraged chickens, snakes that haven't been named) say, "Yes Sir!" when they meet you?

7. To misquote Stephen Colbert, "Do others frequently say, 'You are the epitome of *elephantness.*'?"

If you go to the local bookstore and look for the leadership section you may find hundreds of titles that proclaim the author has identified a number (usually from one through fifty) of the critical characteristics of leadership. Here are a few of those books listed in order by the number of critical characteristics, laws, taboos, etc. in the title:

- *The 1 Thing You Need to Know* — Marcus Buckingham
- *Level 3 Leadership* — James G. Clawson
- *The 5 Dysfunctions of A Team: A Leadership Fable*
  — Patrick M. Lencioni
- *Quiet Leadership: 6 Steps to Transforming Performance at Work* — David Rock
- *The 7 Myths of Knowledge Management* — Marc Rosenburg
- *The 10 Commandments* — God as told to Moses
- *The 17 Irrefutable Laws of Teamwork* — John C. Maxwell
- *The 21 Irrefutable Laws of Leadership* — John C. Maxwell
- *The Message of Leadership: 31 Essential Insights from Proverbs* — Eugene H. Peterson

You get the idea. This is just a handful of the hundreds of books on leadership and coaching that are available today. Marketing departments at publishing houses feel it is important to have a number in the title. I guess they feel we are more likely to believe what the author says and buy the book if there are a finite number of laws to learn. It also helps to have an adjective like *irrefutable*, which is a way to claim victory before you've made the argument.

So how do we learn leadership? Leadership and coaching books can help. Two of the best I've read are *On Becoming A Leader* by Warren Bennis and *The Leadership Challenge* by Jim Kouzes and Barry Posner. But before you get on eBay and try to snipe a bargain, read this quote by Warren Bennis:

"Leadership cannot be taught but it can be learned."

I believe the same is true with coaching. *We learn to coach by coaching and then reflecting upon that experience.* That is why I am supportive of universities hiring people for head coaching positions who have already been a head coach at another level. There are things that you learn being the head coach of a high school team or a junior college team that you cannot learn being the top assistant coach for an NCAA Division I university.

When you are a head coach early in your career you are put in a position to take risks, partly because the program you are directing probably does not have a great tradition, great resources, or great talent. If they did they wouldn't have hired you.

Here are some of the situations I encountered during my first head coaching experience at Louisburg College, a two-year college, in Louisburg, North Carolina, where I was more prepared to teach a course in twentieth century American poetry than I was to develop a collegiate volleyball program from scratch.

• For the 1977 fall season, no one who came out for the team had played organized volleyball, or organized anything for that matter. We began the season with one volleyball, a Tachikara SV5-W, that we guarded like Ark of the Covenant.

• There was no travel budget and on the few occasions we needed to stay overnight we slept on the floor in sleeping bags in the opponent's locker room. Meals on the road were pre-packed pimento cheese sandwiches. When we traveled to the NJCAA National Championships in Miami by bus, we took quarts of milk and orange juice with us from the school cafeteria to save money.

• We had two players over five foot seven and we didn't block for a year and a half.

• The head of the North Carolina AIAW Volleyball Officials believed it was physically impossible to back set without lifting the ball, in effect removing the term "right side player" from the game when she was assigned to a match.

• Our setter became catatonic in the first pool play match of the national championship in 1978. The only thing that covered less distance than her hands, which remained in an arthritic clutch below her chin, were her feet, which squatted motionless like two baked potatoes in an oven.

• Our earnest but elderly bus driver had the annoying habit of exiting off the interstate into the oncoming traffic of the on-ramp. Players took turns riding shotgun behind hoping to reduce the number of potential collisions.

• The starting setter for the first match of organized volleyball at Louisburg College threatened to quit the team while standing in my office on the third floor of Old Main on the eve of the match. I handled the situation as calmly as I could by telling her if she did not recant I would throw her out the third floor window. If she wanted to quit after the match that was her choice. Her other choice was to become the victim in a murder investigation. She never did quit, and today she continues to be a high school coach, hopefully with an office on the first floor.

The three years I spent as head volleyball coach at Louisburg College may be the most important three years in my development, and yet I would be hard pressed to come up with a finite number of rules I could give to a beginning coach from that experience. Instead let me share this from Stephanie Thater, a three-time All-American who recently had her jersey retired at the University of Nebraska. As she and I were standing before a packed house honoring her achievement, she leaned over and whispered, "Do you remember what you used to say to me every time you passed me on the court during practice?" I confessed that I didn't. She said, "You would walk by me close enough that no one else could hear and say, *'Thater, figure it out!'*." And in one way or another that continues to be my mantra when I work with coaches today.

WHERE IN THE WORLD IS
CHRIS BIGELOW?

I am writing this as my wife and I are at 32,000 feet, flying home from watching our daughter play in the Asics President's Day Classic presented by Alegent Health Sports and hosted by Nebraska Elite and Midwest Volleyball Warehouse. That's almost enough sponsorship to fill up the hood of a NASCAR truck and for good reason. More than 300 teams participated in the junior volleyball event, each of them with the attendant pit crew of grandparents, fathers focused on scholarships while manning camcorders, and mothers shepherding younger siblings who are chewing on funnel cakes while wearing tournament t-shirts that will disintegrate before they can be donated to local charities.

On the interstate below our plane our daughter is traveling by motor coach with forty-five other players and coaches on the return leg of a nineteen hour round-trip bus ride. It is the most democratic of American modes of transportation in that when the journey is over, there is the feeling that everyone (on the bus at least) *is* created equal. Three nights of sleeping in a hotel with six players to a room served as a cauldron for bonding and a hot house for influenza.

The tournament itself is a marvel of efficiency. Matches begin on time. Scores are posted within minutes of the completion of each competition. Every court has a new official Mikasa Olympic volleyball that is so soft that you don't know whether to serve it or lie down and take a nap with blue and yellow swirls cradled beneath your ear.

The referees, who do a great job adjusting to the level of play, are the same referees that have been officiating events like this for the past twenty-five years. Someone should do an actuarial study on the life span of U.S.A. Volleyball officials. I think their temperament allows them to rival the longevity of those South American tribes living at 12,000 feet.

Our daughter's team played in the club division with forty-six other teams, which means somewhere in a four-state region there is a Dodge Caravan that missed a turn. Her team played ten matches in three days with at least half of them against teams affiliated with a large junior club in Minnesota. It seems like they had a 15-2, 15-3, 15-silver, 15-Kirby Puckett and a 15-MOA (Mall of America) team all playing in the club division.

The club division is defined by teams that did not get their registration in on time to be in the open division, teams that have head coaches who wear sweatshirts that identify them as "COACH," or teams still in search of a base position.

I have a friend who is a collegiate head coach who tells me that it is very difficult for her to watch the 15's level because all of the kids look the same. I know what she means. *Their mistakes all look the same.* For six minutes each match, talent, training, genes, and intention all come together in a complex integration that looks just like volleyball. The rest of the time it is a slow implosion fueled by feet trying to catch up with brains or a lack of focus running interference for random training. It is a festival of unforced errors.

Lurking at the nets that partition each court is a cadre of college coaches hoping to find someone Chris Bigelow hasn't seen. Cal assistant Bigelow is considered by many of her peers to be the best evaluator of potential college talent, mostly because she spends more time doing it and is more disciplined about it than anyone else. She is rumored to be at this tournament but I have not seen her because Cal, nor recruiters from anywhere else, have 15 clubs on their *"to do"* list.

The head coaches in attendance are like lions as they stake out a piece of turf between a trash can and the tripod of number twelve's uncle. They are mostly by themselves but occasionally they will bring a posse of one assistant coach to ride by their side, someone to talk to so they don't have to interact with their peers.

The culture of the younger assistant coaches is different. They are gregarious, gather in groups, and are eager to share information that is not forbidden by the head coach. Their loyalty to their generation is as strong as their loyalty to the schools that they coach for. Later they will gather in pubs trading tips on job openings with the same deftness that they enter information on their Blackberrys. Many of the second assistants are only a year or two out of school themselves and have more in common with the kids they are evaluating than with the head coach back at mission control.

The focal point for the coaches comes late in the second day when the word has spread that a new club from Texas has black athletes with size and live arms, and the coaches are not yet affiliated with a school that has been to an NCAA Final Four. In other words the club directors are too new to act as agents and are eager to talk with anyone regardless of pedigree. It is a court that will have twice as many coaches as parents, but where in the world is Chris Bigelow? My guess is that she has already identified and evaluated these kids and is boarding a flight to Dayton, Ohio, or Las Vegas. Her biggest challenge is not discovering talent but covering her tracks as other coaches who do not want to work as hard try to follow her path.

By 3:00 p.m. on the final day fatigue has pinned everyone to the mat. The officials stop blowing their whistles, and parents don't have the energy to complain about calls. The few assistant coaches hanging on the dividers look like they got off a train at the wrong stop. The only people moving just as fast as when the tournament began are wearing Hawaiian shirts at Maui Wowi concessions, who consider this weekend a Super Bowl of sorts. Mikasa may have run out of Olympic volleyballs to sell, and Nike may not have women's size six, but by God, Maui Wowi still has flavored corn syrup and bananas, and who doesn't need a pick me up now?

Chris Bigelow retired from coaching and recruiting, January 12, 2011.

THE THREE Rs OF COACHING

The three Rs of coaching are *recruiting, requiring,* and *relating.* While that seems simple enough, it is no less challenging than saying an Alaskan bush pilot needs to take off, maintain consistent air speed, and land safely. Two out of three won't do you much good.

Recruiting can be broken down into two separate but equally-important components. Successful coaches recruit extraordinary talent to their teams. They also recruit players, administrators. and a community to a vision of the culture they are working to create. They recruit players to embrace a specific role; they recruit financial support so that a team can host a competitive tournament; they recruit a director of athletics to become emotionally engaged with the program. Coaching *is* recruiting.

Behind every successful high school program is a coach who has recruited the best athletes to choose the sport they are coaching. In the beginning they do not have much to sell beyond their own energy and enthusiasm. In time, they can recruit to the success and tradition of the program they helped create.

The currency of recruiting is time. While some coaches may have more resources or a more extensive background in recruiting than others, very few programs turn around, make a significant jump, or maintain dominance without a coaching staff investing more hours in recruiting than the competition.

Requiring is what many people associate with coaching. Coaches identify and train behaviors that will give their team the best chance to be successful. Extraordinary coaches are able to do this with a limited amount of drama. Intuitive coaches understand the difference between style and fundamental; between what needs to be changed and what is incidental to the trained behavior.

Requiring championship behaviors is the most critical step in developing a culture. *Repetition is the currency.*

How do we identify championship behaviors? Ask yourself how your team keeps itself from reaching its goals, and then identify the behaviors that address those issues.

If recruiting is not where we want it to be then what changes do we need to make so that we can be more successful?

If we are the worst-serving team in the conference and we need to be the best-serving team in the conference to be competitive, what behaviors will we have to commit to change that dynamic?

If the issues are technical, we will need to commit more time to individual work.

If the issue is a lack of focus, we will need to create specific routines for each player.

If the issue is mental toughness, we will need to create pressure in practice and train players how to deal with it. Each of these behaviors involves a time commitment. At the developmental level, which includes everything from junior high through collegiate competition, change only happens with repetition.

How successful a coaching staff is in *relating* to a team and the individuals on a team can be the determining factor on whether or not a team falls short of, meets, or exceeds expectations.

Here are some observations on behaviors that lead to a healthy and productive relationship between coaches and players:

1. All great leadership begins with hope. There is nothing more powerful than a coach who is able to persuade an individual or a team that they have the right stuff to get the job done if they commit to specific behaviors.

2. Players want consistency more than anything else from the coaching staff. *Consistent communication of expectations and behaviors is the currency of creating a coaching relationship.*

3. The most important question to ask in a player's development is: how does she learn? Many players learn by watching video or having another player model a fundamental. Some players learn through verbal communication, while others have a desire to figure things out for themselves. Some use the left side of their brain to process information and some use the right side of their brain. Some hear information as judgment and have to be taught how to be receptive to new information.

4. The second most important question to ask is: what motivates this player? Until we know what motivates her we may have difficulty in helping her to be uncomfortable enough to risk learning new behaviors.

   How do we learn what a player is motivated by? We ask and listen. The act of listening to a player tells her that we are in this together.

   Listening is the most difficult behavior for some coaches. When we watch the most experienced and successful coaches, such as professional basketball coaches or international volleyball coaches, they spend most of their energy during competition listening (observing) rather than being engaged in frantic directing.

Recruiting, requiring, and relating are critical in developing an extraordinary team, but of the three, recruiting is like oxygen. Without successful recruiting a head coach won't get the opportunity to require and relate for long.

A head coach is not likely to have extraordinary talent in both requiring and relating. She needs to get better in whatever she perceives as her weakness while recruiting an assistant coach who has talent in the area she is trying to get better at. Three coaches on a coaching staff who are all exceptional relaters but deficient in requiring makes for a great end of the year banquet, but there may not be much success on the court to celebrate; three coaches who are great trainers but deficient in relating may run the risk of potential burnout as the season moves to closure.

COACHING AND THE BLACK DOG

From 1984 through 1986 I coached the University of Nebraska volleyball team while battling depression. During that time Nebraska won its first NCAA Regional final, advanced to the NCAA Final Four, and became the first team east of the Rocky Mountains to play for the NCAA National Championship. Not coincidentally, it marked a period of my professional life when I made significant strides as a coach.

The reasons for the depression were some of the usual suspects. My marriage to a high school sweetheart was disintegrating. While counseling was giving me insight into myself and helping to develop skills that would help me with coaching, it was not resulting in a hopeful future for the marriage which ultimately ended following a long separation.

The depression, at times, was disabling. I have heard others refer to it as "the black dog" which follows you wherever you go. When you are in the worst of it you cannot imagine it will get better. It is a struggle to maintain any sense of hope. My apartment was defined by what it didn't have: no plants, photographs, pets, bookcases, draperies, or art. With the exception of the three days a week when my daughter would join me, the only time that I wasn't consumed with my own fear and anger was when I was coaching volleyball. Sometimes I would watch TV and see celebrities talk intimately about their own history of depression and how they moved through it. They did it tentatively though, as if they didn't want to wake it up.

There are some things that accompanied my own depression which were not bad. Some of my senses seemed more alert, and some of the things that might normally have alarmed me made me more curious than afraid. One June evening as I was driving south on Highway 83 toward Wichita, Kansas, a dramatic thunderstorm spread across the sky. Every station on the radio was chirping with warnings of tornadoes, high winds, and sheets of rain, and yet I found the crackling and smell of lightning invigorating. There were two things that helped me move through depression without harming myself or staying depressed longer than I did: first were the conversations I had on a weekly basis with a caring therapist named Frank Brown, who helped me move from intense fear and anxiety toward positive decisions and actions. The second was the challenge of coaching volleyball.

In the spring of 1985 we had graduated two setters, Mary Buysee and Cathy Noth, who had been at the core of a 6-2 offense and our success during the previous three seasons. Both would go on to successful careers in college coaching, Mary as the head coach at South Dakota State and Cathy as my assistant coach at Nebraska following several years as a player with the U.S. National Team. The heir apparent to the setter position was Tisha Delaney, a five foot eight junior college transfer who had received almost no individual training in the fall, and because she had redshirted, had no playing time.

At a breakfast following our elimination from the 1984 NCAA Regional tournament in Kellogg, Michigan, one of the returning starters volunteered the opinion that the future of Nebraska volleyball was pretty dim primarily because of Tisha's lack of consistency. When I overheard this remark, I ushered the player into an adjoining room where I told her that, "If I ever heard her question the abilities of one of her teammates in the future she would be lucky to find herself sitting on the bench next to me; and that Tisha would be a great setter on a great team, possibly a team without the right side player who I was presently talking to."

This was an interesting conversation for two reasons: one, because I spoke so loudly everyone in the other room could hear me; and two, because I had some reservations and doubts about Tisha being able to do the job myself. But in the midst of a hangover from a devastating loss the night before, in a small airport café before boarding an even smaller plane for a fog-bound flight across Lake Michigan to Chicago, I moved out of depression long enough to pin a player to the wall with a fierce commitment to do everything I possibly could to make sure that Tisha would become a great setter.

While Tisha was not a polished setter, she was not without toughness and talent. Her father died when she was very young and she had developed the competiveness of a survivor. She had attended Jefferson Community College where she played for Jo Ellen Stringer, a caring coach who would accumulate more wins than any other coach in junior college history.

Tisha had quick feet, large hands, and, as we would learn during the next two seasons, was a fierce competitor. What she didn't have was consistent contact with the ball. The ball stayed in her hands a long time before waffling out in arcs too unpredictable for an up-tempo offense.

For an hour each day we met in the Nebraska Coliseum where I tossed balls and Tisha learned to set: first against the wall, occasionally to a teammate, but mostly back to me while I stood on a wooden box. One thousand sets a day with specific footwork allowed her to develop into a setter who would become an AVCA All-American and lead her team to a national championship match.

With each toss from the box, my anger diminished for a few seconds. With each step of her development I began to focus less on my own despair and more on building a team that could compete for a championship. I gradually, and painfully, replaced depression with the positive addiction of coaching.

I do not want to make this sound easier than it was: fighting depression is the toughest battle I have ever faced. Had I not felt the responsibility to be a good parent, or had I not had the support of a wonderful counselor, I might have given up. But here is another truth: the battle made me a better coach. My feelings were more intense. I developed more empathy for the people around me. The development of players became personal, as if they were the wave that would give me the opportunity to save myself. And as I coached, I swam.

DEEP VOLLEYBALL THOUGHTS

• When the second official comes over to tell you that you have already used your timeouts, tell him you thought they were free, like molecules in the air. It won't keep you from getting a yellow card, but it will give him something to think about for the rest of the match.

• You know how some players keep hitting the ball into the bottom of the block, over and over? It reminds me of that Greek guy who kept trying to push a rock up a hill and it kept rolling back on him. Except the Greek guy wasn't on scholarship.

• You want to have real fun with your team? Turn in the wrong lineup. Flip-flop a middle attacker with an outside hitter. You won't believe the look in the players' eyes. And then, one of them will say, "Here we go again."

• When a junior coach tells you one of his players is too good to play for your school you can respond "old school" by putting a potato in the tail pipe of his limousine; or you can respond "new school" by trying to put a potato up his ass. Either way is not too good for the potato.

• If you really want to deflate an outside hitter who is playing with too much confidence, you can call her by a different name, like Shirley. But if her real name is Shirley this won't work because you have to have a lot of confidence anyway to play with a name like that.

• If your back row setter tries to sneak into the front row before you substitute, you can admire her courage and ambition or you can say ,"Listen here squirt, we aren't playing any little people in the front row." Unless she really is a little person, in which case you should probably just let her go ahead.

• If someone calls you up and asks you to put the phone in the waste basket because it is raining and they want to drain the phone lines, it is probably a prank call or your assistant coach trying to see if you have a sense of humor following a tough loss. You can find out by just setting the receiver down for an hour or so. If no one is on it when you return it was probably just a prank call.

• If you are embarrassed about not having a lion or a wolverine for a mascot, at least your team isn't named after a kitchen utensil. You know something like "the Fighting Can Openers" or "the Enraged Colanders." That would be hard to overcome.

• If you lose a match after your team was ahead 2-0, you can look at the stat sheet and try to find out what you could have done differently, or you can just blame everything on the setter. Either way no one is going to sit next to you on the bus ride home.

TRUST, COACHING BEHAVIORS, AND THE DUCK IN THE BALCONY

A coach who doesn't trust himself can never really trust his players.

One goal on every coach's checklist is to have his or her team play its best volleyball at the end of the season. So what can a head coach do to develop this characteristic? Here are some possibilities:

1. Teams that finish the season with great play are able to develop trust between the starting setter and the head coach. Setting is the most demanding position, not just because the setter touches the ball the most or that she can elevate her teammates with her own play, but because she is charged with carrying out the head coach's game plan. This is very difficult to do if there is interference between the head coach and the setter. If a setter is going to take the necessary risks that lead to success on the court, she can't be spending energy on wondering whether or not her head coach believes in her.

2. Nothing energizes a team in the latter part of the season like the dramatic emergence of a talented attacker. While she may have been tentative earlier in the season, she is now energized by success and confidence that allows a coaching staff to develop tactical adjustments based on her development. The difference between having one dynamic offensive player and two cannot be measured on a base-10 system. A Richter scale would be more appropriate.

3. Some coaches spend a majority of practice in opponent preparation during the latter half of a conference season. There are several reasons for this. One of them is watching too much video which leads to focusing almost exclusively on the next opponent at the expense of player development. If a coach wants a team to play its best volleyball at the end of the year she has to continue to teach and provide the time for repetitions that allow players to get better. *If a team goes three days without practicing a specific fundamental, that movement or behavior is going to deteriorate and impact future matches.*

4. The best programs keep polishing their strengths, particularly the characteristics that make them unique. What makes Long Beach State difficult to prepare for is the tempo of their passing. It requires the opposing blockers and backcourt defenders to process information quicker than they are comfortable with. Opponents get one or two days to prepare for the geometry of the 49ers' ball handling. But if Long Beach is working on it every day, the difference between what they are doing and the opponent's preparation is even greater later in the season. *Anything a team can do that is unique to their system is an advantage in late season play.*

5. The quirks of scheduling, injuries, and fatigue mean that almost every team is going to experience a disappointing loss or desultory play during the second half of the season. What may be more important is how the head coach responds to his own anxiety about disappointing performances. Everything needs to be addressed in terms of behaviors, not personalities. Individual work and shorter practices may help. What players do not need is lengthy team meetings filled with neurotic, rhetorical questions.

6. One way for a coach to reduce his own anxiety and do a better job making adjustments during a match is to develop a checklist of observations to focus on. Most opponents reveal their tactical game plan very early in a match. A series of questions could include:
    *   Are the opponent's base and release defenses the same as our scouting report?

- Is the opponent tracking our middle attackers in transition?
- Is the opponent committing blockers in certain rotations?
- Is there a duck in the balcony?

Thinking about anything is better than hyperventilating on what it would mean to win or lose this match. Success is more likely when a head coach models the behaviors he would like from his players as the pressure rises.

7. Every team has a specific opponent it is going to have to defeat to reach its goal, whether that be winning a national championship or defeating their traditional rival. In 1996 I believed if we were fortunate enough to advance to the NCAA Division I Final Four, we would eventually have to play Stanford which had a covey of great players, including Kerri Walsh who was even more effective from the back row than she was from the front row.

I committed ten minutes at the end of each practice in the second half of the season to having our defense transition from attacks by our male assistant who approached off a two-foot box to simulate the angle of Walsh's back row attacks. Only the coaching staff knew what we were preparing for. As luck would have it, we did advance to the semifinals where we met, and were defeated in four games by, the eventual national champion Stanford team. Even though we lost the match we were competitive because we had prepared for something our schedule could not simulate.

8. The biggest confidence booster is when a team comes from behind to win a match which appeared to have been lost. When this happens the winning team carries a feeling of invincibility and joy into the next competition that sometimes carries into the postseason. I would not, however, suggest losing the first two games of the next match to position your team for a transformational experience. There will be plenty of other opportunities to exercise patience and leadership in the second half of the conference season as the arbitrary challenges of injuries, indifference, and fatigue show up like eager trick-or-treaters. Happy Halloween.

TERRY PETTIT

THE LONGHORN LIMOUSINE

2009 Ride of the Year: A review of this year's makes and models

The Longhorn Limousine SE with leather package:
The Longhorn Limousine SE is a 1977 Lincoln Continental, but with marble floors and a sunroof that allows Destinee Hooker to stretch her six foot four frame whenever she wants to tip "*biqs*" to the crowd. The car is driven by six foot three Ashlee Engle who may be the best all-around volleyball player in the Big 12 Conference, but as of this writing was in the setter position where she doesn't have the opportunity to pass or attack from the right side, two talents Texas needs to improve on in order to compete for a national championship. The lady waving from the window is head coach, Jerritt Elliott's top recruit, assistant coach Salima Rockwell, a former setter and assistant coach at Penn State who brings a noticeable presence to the already talented Longhorn Limo.

The Husky GMC Squared Jimmy:
The finest Husky and Mormon engineering have combined to make the first armored GMC Squared Jimmy out of the University of Washington. Inside, head coach Jim McLaughlin squints as he monitors fourteen computers that spew out information on mileage, dump probability, the propensity to run a crossing pattern in the third rotation, and a voice-over extolling the virtues of swing blocking (why hasn't someone figured out that the best way to attack this strategy is by running a swing offense?). I digress, but Washington doesn't. "Jimmy Mac" trains outside hitters better than anyone else in the women's game.

The Husky offense is deceptively quick and clean, and their defense is good enough to win a national championship against anybody residing outside the State College city limits.

The Stanford Tie-Dyed School Bus:
The acid-colored, camouflaged school bus with the most annoying mascot in collegiate sport is driven by an Opie Taylor look-alike, John Dunning of Stanford, one of the best coaches in the country at working with difficult and talented athletes. The Cardinal volleyball team usually takes blue highways until halfway through the season when Coach Dunning and crew have the right people in the right seats to win the toughest conference. Like any of the teams ranked from three to thirty-three, Stanford's best chance to visit Tampa is to avoid an early hookup with Penn State in the Western Regional, which Stanford is hosting.

The Wahine Hybrid:
Powered by trade winds and the karma of lei-covered fans, Hawaii could float into Tampa with more miles than the rest of the field combined. If Hawaii doesn't make the Final Four it won't be from jet lag, but from a conference schedule that challenges the coaching staff to prepare for a level of play they haven't seen since early season play. Hawaii travels best when it has home-grown talent like five foot eleven outside hitters Kanani Danielson and Aneli Cuba-Otineru as well as five foot ten setter Dani Mafua.

The Cadillac Escalade Nittany:
Penn State's ride is the biggest, baddest Cadillac Escalade ever, with tinted windows and an extra compartment on top where head coach Russ Rose sits with a fine Cuban cigar watching video of the pit drill he has run in every practice since 1979. Extra wide white-walled tires, and a 2,000 rpm, Megan Hodge-powered engine belies the fact that the Escalade Nittany can go off-road when it has to and grovel with the best of them. I don't know which is more impressive, Penn State's team attack percentage at .421 or Penn State's opponent attack percentage at .094. Opponents speak in tongues about the rare achievement of getting Penn State to call a timeout.

Others who could gather on the beach for the green flash:

- There are not any rock stars in Lincoln, Nebraska, but there is a very good player at every position and if the lion lottery doesn't pick Omaha, they have as good a chance as anyone outside Happy Valley.
- When the Pax-10 frat pack isn't pointing fingers at each other they are comfortable playing and beating the best: Trojans, Ducks, and Bears, oh my!
- Mary Wise, full-time head coach and part time cheerleader at the University of Florida, mentors Kelly Murphy, the best player south of Megan Hodge.
- Minnesota is a regional host and has one of the best on the bench in Mike Hebert, but lost one of the Gophers' best with Brook Dieter's departure.
- Iowa State's Christy Johnson understands the value of going 22-8 and winning at the right time.
- Michigan, with Mark Rosen at the helm, took Penn State to five sets, something only two teams have done in the past two years.
- Brian Gimmillaro's Long Beach State is like a Jaguar XKE. It's in the garage for much of the time, but when it's running nothing purrs better.
- Kentucky, LSU, Florida State, Baylor, Illinois, Texas A&M, Notre Dame, and Colorado State have enough horsepower to draft through an early round or two if they race each other.

Any team that is not in Penn State's bracket could join the lion-feast in Tampa. But let's not go "balloon boy" here; if you wanted to beat Penn State you needed to do it two years ago when the setter was inexperienced and the ball handling wasn't great. Rose, Hodge, Alisha Glass, Blair Brown, Arielle Wilson, Darcy Dorton, Alyssa D'Errico, and those sixteen defensive specialists are too good to make a detour now. So sit back and light up a Cohiba for a great college volleyball team as it brushes aside expectations, interference, and sixty-three well-coached teams to win its third consecutive national championship.

TERRY PETTIT

THE ANATOMY OF A
GREAT CHAMPIONSHIP

Champions keep playing until they get it right. — Billie Jean King

Texas	(2)	25 25 23 21 13	29-2
Penn State	(3)	22 20 25 25 15	38-0

There is an old saw in coaching that says "to win a national championship you are going to have win at least one match when you don't play your best." Consider the following from the 2009 NCAA Division I Volleyball Championship Match:

• Penn State's six foot three outside hitter Megan Hodge, the two-time AVCA National Player of the Year, had the last kill of the national championship match to lift her attack percentage for the night to .137 on seventy-three attempts, .240 below her season average.

• Penn State's M1, Arielle Wilson, who hit a sick .540 for the year, had nine kills but was limited to only twenty-three attempts for the night, while six foot five teammate Blair Brown, whom many considered the best right side attacker in the country, was hitting .125 at the end of game two, before rallying to finish at .257, almost .100 percentage points below her season average.

On the Texas side of the net:

• Texas senior left side hitter, six foot four Destinee Hooker, a three-time NCAA high jump champion, had thirty-four kills in a performance which could best be described as "Labronesque."

The angles of her attack were so severe, that combined with the remarkable floor defense played by both teams the championship match was elevated to high theater.

• AVCA All-American setter/hitter Ashley Engle compiled eight kills, thirty-six assists, and wielded an aggressive top-spin jump-serve that had Penn State on its heels early, while Texas' five foot nine senior libero Heather Kisner had the match of her life, throwing her body in front of Penn State missiles, like the digital flippers in a video game to finish with a match-leading twenty six-digs.

Texas finished with ten more kills, out-hit Penn State .251 to .234, and on this night, had the best player on the court. So how did the Nittany Lions win?

• Enter three Nittany Lions stage right: five foot one defensive specialist junior Cathy Quilico and five foot nine junior libero Alyssa D'Errico combined for thirty-three digs and four aces, and Penn State's fourth option on attack, six foot three freshman outside hitter Darcy Dorton, had thirteen kills while playing with the freedom and the enthusiasm that comes from having an insurance policy named Megan Hodge in the H1 position.

• D'Errico and Quilico not only passed, defended, and covered their attackers at Nintendo-like speed, they were also Penn State's most efficient and forcing servers; Quilico with a tough left-handed line-to-line floater to zone 1, and D'Errico with a quiver of jump top-spin and float serves she could alternate with the countenance of a ninja warrior.

Both of them came up with service runs which allowed Penn State to get up off the mat. If ever there was a match that showed why coaches should be investing scholarships in liberos, this was the match.

In the first two sets, Texas was the pursuer with Hooker proving why she is the best closer in college volleyball. Several times in her career she has taken over a set when the odometer reaches twenty, frequently turning attacks from bump-sets and difficult approaches into signature moments. She did exactly that in set one, finishing with the final three kills, the last off one foot from the back row that would require a protractor to chart. In the second set she had eleven kills, one more than the entire Penn State team.

Sometimes when two teams with equal talent and skill go to battle, the team who makes the last successful adjustment wins.

Penn State head coach Russ Rose rotated Brown into the front row to match up with Hooker at the start of the third set; and the Penn State blockers began to get more touches while the back row defenders began to adjust to the advanced geometry of Hooker's attacks. (In sets one and two Hooker had sixteen kills with a .550 kill percentage. In sets three and four she had thirteen kills with a .320 kill percentage. But what may be even more important is *when* she got her kills. In the two sets that Texas won, Hooker had the final six kills for both teams. In the three sets that Penn State won, she had fewer attempts with two kills and two errors in the endgame.)

In set three, Penn State took leads of 22–17 and 24–20, only to have the Longhorns rally to close at 24–23. Hooker swung to tie the score but D'Errico, now releasing to a ridiculous thirteen feet off the net at angle, dug the ball to left front where Hodge attacked the second ball inside the Texas block, for a Penn State win at 25-23.

Defense, aggressive serving, seven kills from Hodge, and four Texas service errors enabled Penn State to win the fourth set, 25- 21, despite hitting only .181. In the final set with setter extraordinaire Alisha Glass distributing the ball to Brown, Wilson, Hodge, and Dorton, Penn State countered Hooker's five kills and put itself in position to win its third consecutive national championship. Engle delayed the celebration by siding-out on a set from Michelle Kocher to bring the set to 14-13, Penn State. Engle then unleashed an aggressive jump-serve that seemed to promise an opportunity to tie the score on an overpass, but a joust at the net and a recovery by Glass allowed Wilson to bump-set Hodge, whose attack split the Texas block and scurried past Hooker for the match-winning kill.

The Penn State players responded with both joy and relief as they toppled onto the court. Despite the talk about playing one set, one point, at a time, the knowledge of being in position to do something that no other NCAA Division I women's college volleyball team has done can create an interference that lives in one's synapses.

Much of the conversation as people were leaving the arena was centered on Hooker and her amazing match and personal gifts. Lost in the buzz was the obvious: it is incredibly hard to win one national championship; three in a row takes luck, extraordinary athletes, great coaching, and an almost Biblical resistance to injuries, sickness, and pestilence.

Penn State won its third consecutive national championship with its 101st consecutive win in what is safe to say, was its most challenging victory in a journey that has prompted opposing coaches to exhaust the synonyms for dominant, athletic, and well-coached. They did it by doing what all great champions do: they endured.

THE BARKING IN THE ARENA

We don't talk about them much. The players who are out of sync, who don't seem to get it, who seem to have no joy in the process of becoming a better team. Those players might include:

- The gifted player who flips-off officials, ignores her teammates, and baits the opponent.
- The outside hitter who celebrates wildly with only her own successes.
- The AVCA All-American who pouts her way through a championship match because a younger teammate is recognized at a banquet.
- The opponent who will go on to star in the Olympics, but ignores a senior teammate who is being honored for her standout career.
- The talented athlete who works hard to become a player and then stops, coasting through a senior season of disappointment and regret.
- The rumors of a team that commits to lose a conference championship because it was the only way they believed they could get back at a controlling coach.
- The tremendous talent who is only interested in her teammates when they can do something for her.
- The great players who chose isolation over courage.

- The team captain who substitutes manipulation for leadership.
- The players who ask for their stats following a gut-wrenching loss.
- The player who signals from the bench for someone to rescue her with lip-gloss or refill her bottle with water.
- The player who drains everyone else with constant complaining and a rationing of passion.
- The player who only responds to the head coach and dismisses her peers.
- The player who is on a life mission to drain everyone around her of energy.

We don't talk about them because they do not make for good stories or teammates. But the truth is, they command a good deal of our time. We want them to feel the joy of being part of something beyond their personal goals.

We want them to know what it feels like to look across the huddle into the eyes of a teammate and know that you will not quit because you will not let each other down.

We want them to understand that while it is possible to win without friendship, teamwork, and countenance with others, it is a journey without much texture or depth.

We want them to know there is no trust without vulnerability.

We want them to know that years from now what they will miss may not be championships or ribbons, trophies with their nameplates, All-American certificates, or recognition.

What they will miss, the volleyball alumnae tell us, is coming into the arena at 3:00 p.m., and knowing no matter how their day has gone with calculus, accounting, and misunderstandings with a roommate, they have this community of purpose; a community that does not spend energy in saying we are different or special, or that wears t-shirts with slogans proclaiming you wish you were us. It is a community whose goals are important, but perhaps nothing is more important than the barking of "Hellos," "How are you?", "Let's pepper," and knowing you are part of the pack.

Sometimes years later, they may send a note or call by long distance to tell us how they have come to an understanding of what they missed. It is a unique club when you are willing to set aside some of your personal dreams and culture to become part of a pack that for hours each day hunts with each other for those few moments when communication, sweat, synapses, and effort combine to form the ultimate moment in sport where commitment dances with trust.

There may be no more frustrating feeling for a coach than when he cannot figure out how to reach someone who doesn't get it. But this is one of the things we signed up for. Coaching is not limited to training, strategy, and tactical decisions. It is not about being understood or appreciated. It is about knocking on a door every day, until one day the player on the other side, opens it and says, "I'm ready."

TERRY PETTIT

DELIVERANCE, VOLCANOES, AND JOURNEYS

In May 1975, five graduate students in creative writing prepared to bed down for the night in a barn loft just above the banks of the Buffalo River in north central Arkansas.

As we unrolled our sleeping bags onto the wide pine planks of the loft, we talked about the recently released movie *Deliverance*, and the canoe trip we would begin in the morning on one of the most beautiful and wild rivers in America. This trip was only possible because spring rains provided enough water to prevent having to portage the upper sections of the Buffalo, and enough clearance to make the rapids navigable downstream.

The woman unrolling her sleeping bag next to me was Carolyn Wright, a classmate in the poetry workshop who would later go on to a prominent career as a poet. Decadent in the best sense of the word, Carolyn told interesting gothic stories about her childhood, and while many of us in the workshop focused on trying to say something meaningful, she had the talent and good sense to focus on language that was as rich as liquor.

For a while we discussed James Dickey's screenplay and whether or not the violence that occurs in *Deliverance* was an accurate depiction of the Deep South. Most of us thought some of the characters bordered on caricatures, even though they gave shape to the sense of evil that permeates the novel and makes a flawed movie one of the few I have watched several times over. One of us observed if you've ever been in a canoe with a friend or lover, you know trouble doesn't come from the outside, but inside the canoe.

Just as we were about to fall asleep, I turned to Carolyn and told her about a book I had read the previous week, Malcolm Lowry's *Under the Volcano*, a novel that held whispered respect among our fiction-writing friends. The story takes place on the Day of the Dead in a small village in Mexico which lies in the shadow of two volcanoes. The main character is an alcoholic English counsel, who hopes to reconcile with his beautiful wife. I will say nothing else about the book other than you must have patience to read it, but if you do, be prepared to go through the windshield in the final pages.

That evening and the following day on the river is the last time that I saw Carolyn that spring. When I returned from a road trip two weeks later, where I found a teaching job in North Carolina, she had read *Under the Volcano*, and left for Mexico the following day, where she stayed for much of the summer in the small village that was the setting for Lowry's novel. I have always thought her response to the novel was one of the most powerful things I had ever heard.

By now you are wondering what this has to do with coaching. There are few things more powerful in our lives than a journey into the unknown. Sometimes the journey is prompted by a story; sometimes it's two weeks in a Volkswagen looking for a job, taking on a river in a canoe, or a trip to Mexico.

The journey and the time away from the usual concerns is as important in a coach's continuing development as training and recruiting. Each time we put ourselves in a new geography with different metaphors and language, we learn a little more about who we are, and when we return we are better prepared to adjust to the challenges we face and move on.

ANOTHER MISSED OPPORTUNITY

My first cell phone was Motorola bag phone that had the heft and design features of a brick. It was 1995 and I made three calls for the year, while receiving none. I didn't memorize the number and I certainly didn't give it out. The last thing I wanted was to have someone call me when I was recruiting or fly-fishing.

I thought about that phone last week as our family considered the options available today, particularly *smart phones* like the iPhone and the DROID. Anne and I had deliberately not upgraded our phones in three years, so when our daughter's two-year contract was in sync with ours, we could consider other cell phone plans like Sprint and AT&T.

I have had several people tell me, with a countenance not unlike lighting a cigarette following sex they believe the iPhone is mankind's greatest invention. Now to be sure, none of these people lived during a plague or polio outbreak, or had personal family members who were part of the Donner Party, but even so, their enthusiasm seemed to make their lack of perspective almost endearing.

When I ask them why they believe an iPhone is a more significant achievement than a Porsche Speedster or a Titleist seven iron, two inventions I am particularly fond of, they inevitably respond because the iPhone already has several hundred thousand applications that have been developed for it.

Beyond (yawn), GPS, calendar, camera, and recording features are clever options I never would have thought of (at least after eighth grade). There is an iFart application. There is a dog whistle and an application you can click to hear your favorite *Star Wars* character say a signature phrase. Before you finish reading this someone will have created an application that sounds like Spock farting while dog whistling at the same time.

There are dating applications for cross-dressers searching for transvestite crane operators. There are applications that can translate your dog's barking into Portuguese. Should you be bitten by a black mamba, there is an application that tells you the five most important things to do. Number five is to bend over and put your head between your legs and kiss your sweet ass goodbye, but only after naming who will inherit your iPhone in the "*i-am-about-to-die*" application.

So how much would it cost to be able to get a device that could reserve a table for four at the L'Esguard restaurant in Sant Andreu de Llavaneres, Spain, where what one iPhone blogger had what she called the worst meal in memory?

I could trade in my customized Sprint Samsung with duct tape holding in the battery (I call it my Samsung Urban Model) for an entry-level iPhone for $200 plus an extra $15 a month for a data plan that would allow me to become more self-absorbed and introverted, especially in public spaces or across the dinner table. For the three of us (i-Abacus please) the total would be $600 plus $45 a month for the life of the plan, plus a one-time upgrade of $25, plus the slight inconvenience of not being able to call anyone in a major American city between four o'clock in the morning and eleven o'clock at night because the call is likely to be dropped since so many iPhone users are using the "*i-stand-by-me*" application which offers opinions on whether or not Goofy is a dog or who would win in a battle between a gorilla and a python.

Which raises an interesting question. Could a python digest a Motorola bag phone? Unfortunately, I don't know the answer because there is only one place that might offer an opinion; and unfortunately I decided on a more modest upgrade to an LG Remarq which only cost me fifty bucks, if you count the $100 rebate, which should show up before the next comet named after a female president lights up the evening sky.

A COACH IN FULL

There are two things that can happen as an exceptional coach moves into the last third of his career: he can get stuck by refusing to adapt or he can make some seemingly small but significant adjustments that allow him to become an even better coach.

Most of us get stuck. We don't alter our vision of how to recruit, train, or play. We push down harder on the unique talent that allowed us to become a good coach in the first place without addressing changes in technique, in the culture, in the size of athlete it takes to compete.

When this happens frustration can turn to anger and we begin explaining our predicament in terms outside of our control. Our lack of success or progress is framed by the conference we're in, the lack of a BCS football team, the kids who aren't coachable, the lack of minorities in our community, or the focus of the athletic department being on women's basketball.

Whether or not a coach has the courage and willingness to adapt will determine if he spends his final seasons talking about kids he coached ten years ago while dumping camp money into a SEP IRA, or putting himself in position to be as uncomfortable as he was when he was a developing coach. If he chooses the latter he may discover a behavior or philosophy that once was beneficial to be at the heart of why he is stuck today.

There are 329 NCAA Division I volleyball programs. If we assume (albeit incorrectly) that each team has equal resources, talent, leadership, strength of schedule, and coaching, the odds of winning the national championship in any given year would be 1 in 329.

The odds of the same team winning four consecutive national championships are 1 in 11,716,114,081. Just for the fun of it, let's say that out loud: One in eleven billion, seven hundred and sixteen million, one hundred and fourteen thousand, and eighty-one.

Of course Division I volleyball is not contested on a level playing field. In thirty years of NCAA women's volleyball tournament competition, only ten schools have won a national title. In some years there are only a handful of teams who have a realistic chance to compete for the title.

As the 2010 season began most people *outside* the Big Ten Conference believed Penn State, with the graduation of All-American setter Alisha Glass and National Player of the Year Megan Hodge (both currently playing with the U.S. National Team), plus a preseason injury to sophomore outside hitter Darcy Dorton, would probably not allow Penn State to contend with preseason favorites Stanford, Nebraska, and Florida.

Big Ten coaches had a different point of view. They were focusing on Penn State's returning All-Americans, senior right side player Blair Brown and senior middle blocker Arielle Wilson, as well as superb floor defenders Alyssa D'Errico and Cathy Quilico. They also knew Penn State would be defending its three consecutive national titles with Russ Rose, the most successful head coach in women's volleyball, while hosting an NCAA Regional Championship in Happy Valley. They made this observation while crossing forefingers in front of their chests.

While the Nittany Lions were training a former defensive specialist, five foot six sophomore Kristin Carpenter, to become the starting setter in a 5-1 system, Stanford, Nebraska, and Florida all decided to run a two-setter offenses which can be as problematic as a turboprop; they both have too many moving parts. The 6-2 systems struggle to maintain a rhythm, are vulnerable to back row attack, and the setters in a 6-2 system have about the same opportunity for leadership as the pusher in a two-man bobsled.

Stanford, Nebraska, and Florida all lost in regional tournaments to teams (USC, Washington, and Purdue) who ran simpler 5-1 systems. The winning teams also made fewer errors and, on that particular night, outplayed their higher-ranked opponents.

In the meantime, Penn State was hosting an NCAA Regional Championship in Rec Hall which did not feature opponents that were on anyone's shortlist (with the exception of the NCAA Volleyball Committee) to advance to the national tournament finals in Kansas City.

In the past two years the committee had gotten the right teams into the tournament, but seemed to have lacked the intuitive intelligence or leadership to place the strongest teams in different brackets.

In Rec Hall, Penn State defeated a competitive, but overmatched Duke squad, 3-1, in the regional finals (the first the Blue Devils had ever competed in) before moving on to Kansas City.

As the 2010 NCAA Final Four approached, Cal appeared to be playing the best volleyball in the country. The Golden Bears defeated the Golden Gophers of Minnesota, 3-0, in the semifinals of the Seattle Regional before dismantling Washington in the finals with a .364 hitting percentage on the Huskies' home court.

USC, who had upset Stanford in the Dayton Regional, had enough young talent to compete with anyone, but had the unenviable task of trying to beat a great conference opponent for the third time in the same year. That dynamic helped the Trojans in Dayton, Ohio, but shifted to Cal's favor in Kansas City.

Cal defeated USC in the second NCAA Final Four semifinal, 3-1, as junior outside hitter Tarah Murrey (twenty-three kills) and senior setter Carli Lloyd both made strong cases for player of the year honors. Murrey had totaled seventy-eight kills in three matches against USC, a team who had beaten the Bears twice and had one of the best tactical coaches in the country in Mick Haley.

The other Final Four semifinal, featuring Penn State and Texas, was the one that drew everyone's attention. As one coach observed, "Texas had been a 'friggin' light show for the second half of the Big 12 season." Head coach Jerritt Elliott said it was the best chemistry of any team he had ever coached. All-American Juliann Faucette's bad-girl routine of the previous two years had evolved into solid leadership. The Longhorns had overwhelmed Big 12 Champion Nebraska in their final conference meeting with a quick-tempo offense that made the Huskers' 6-2 system look like they were playing Mintonette.

In the Austin Regional final the Longhorns overcame an inspired Purdue team that had taken out top-seeded Florida in the regional semifinal, and might have persevered in the final if the Boilersmakers' senior setter and inspirational leader Jaclyn Hart had not succumbed to injury toward the end of the first game.

It was about halfway through the NCAA Final Four semifinal match between Texas and Penn State that 12,000 people suddenly realized, "Oh s&*t they're going to do it again," as the Nittany Lions skated to a 25-13, 25-13, 25-22 victory over the Longhorns with freshman left side hitter Deja McClendon making her Final Four debut with eleven kills, no errors, and a .733 attack percentage.

Almost everyone outside of University Park, Pennsylvania, was hoping for a Cal victory in the final and there was reason for hope. Cal had the best setter in the tournament, and prior to the finals the most effective left side player in the tournament in Murrey.

Cal's head coach, Rich Feller, is one of those coaches who has adapted in his fourteen-year tenure at Cal where he has surrounded himself with talented assistants such as Chris Bigelow and Sam Crossen, and developed one of the top programs in the Pac-10 and Pac-12 Conferences. Taking a team that was not ranked higher than fifth in the 2010 Pac-10 preseason poll to the NCAA Finals earned Feller the AVCA National Coach of the Year Award.

But no one has adapted more in the latter half of this decade than Penn State's Rose. In 2001, just three years after a national championship, the Nittany Lions suffered a rare early exit from the NCAA tournament, losing to Temple, 3-1. Some recruiting mistakes, health issues, and perhaps coaching fatigue had the Nittany Lions on the verge of being stuck.

For years, Penn State's best teams had featured two aircraft carriers, a setter, and three role players. No one liked to coach the overachiever more than Rose, hence a Penn State roster that looked like a mixture of international quarter milers with a club soccer team.

At some point Rose decided he liked competing for national championships more than he liked kids with headbands in the front row. Now, everyone at the net has national team size. Rose, more than any other women's coach, has adapted the simplicity of the men's game to the Nittany Lions' "M.O." The outside sets are deceptively quick, and each attacker focuses on one primary attack. It is an offense built on efficiency and tempo and it works in part because of the ball handling skills of Penn State's liberos and defensive specialists.

Coach Rose has always had the right kids in the right position. He has always trained defense, pursuit, and covering as well as anyone in the game. His players have always been low-error with a great understanding of how Penn State wins. He doesn't get in his players' way and he doesn't put undue expectations on them with hype. He also doesn't create a dependency where they are looking for an emotional handout after each point. He has done all these things throughout his career but in recent years he is doing it with a different breed of cat and at a twenty-first century pace.

Known for sarcasm that can approach cynicism, Rose would be a great guy to have in the foxhole next to you unless you were about to die. He wouldn't tell you what you want to hear. But the sarcasm is softer now and is overshadowed by the simplicity and consistency of his message. Oregon head coach Jim Moore, when asked what Rose does best, said, "Russ has the ability to tell his truth to his players without them rolling their eyes."

There is a saying among coaches that "we need to have our athletes train like women, with great focus and attention to detail, but compete like men." When it counted the most, Penn State played without fear; Cal played as if it was not sure if it could win, leading to a fourth consecutive national championship for Penn State, 25-20, 27-25, 25-20. McClendon, Brown, and Wilson combined for forty-six kills, and McClendon won her first NCAA Finals MVP award.

There are hundreds of reasons why Penn State has achieved its remarkable record in the past four years. The Penn State campus is located less than a day's drive from more than a third of the country's population. Inconsistent support for volleyball on the East Coast has helped Penn State mine some of the extraordinary talent that has graced

State College in recent years, where the nearest volleyball program who has reached a national championship match is over 800 miles away. Hosting a regional helps; upsets help; and the lack of a dominant team all played parts in Penn State's 2010 National Championship. But make no mistake, Penn State's Russ Rose, a coach in full, who is decidedly not stuck, played the largest part.

VOLLEYBALL IN THE RUINS: A SPRING RANT

I retired from coaching at the University of Nebraska in 2000, and didn't plan a practice until recently when I began coaching our daughter's club team in Northern Colorado. Coaching club volleyball while mentoring collegiate coaches has given me the opportunity to see some facets of a game that is increasingly shaped by money or the lack of it.

• Coaches used to wait until an athlete reached puberty before offering a scholarship. I couldn't predict whether or not a prospective player would be as passionate about volleyball as she was about becoming a vegan six years into the future. There is an old saying: "A rising tide lifts all boats." When the rising tide is the *fear of getting shut out*, it lifts unhappy parents, coaches, and players all looking for a better fit three or four years later. It is very expensive to recruit out of fear.

• Some coaches still don't get it right about recruiting setters. Whether or not a setter is a six foot two, left-hander, with a twenty-eight inch vertical jump, is about as important as whether or not a Porsche has a back seat. There are only two accessories worth discussing. Does she win? Does she make the people around her better?

• SIZE has become more important in recruiting than arm speed, vision, balance, hand-eye coordination, and motivation. This could change if collegiate volleyball adopted fewer (eight) substitutions with the libero. It would also result in developing complete players at both the junior and collegiate level. With fifteen subs and a libero, coaches are trying to specialize in every rotation, frequently disrupting the opportunity to develop any sense of rhythm. Six rotation middle players are becoming as rare as senior women administrators with clout.

• The highest concentration of minority volleyball players continues to be on our women's national team. Beyond acknowledging the lack of minorities in our sport, there continues to be no plan from U.S.A. Volleyball to actively address a situation that has been discussed for at least forty years. USAV could do our sport (and its public relations) a lot of good if it prioritized a specific percentage of profits from qualifiers go back into the junior community for the development of minority and low-income junior players.

• Club volleyball is like Afghanistan. It is tribal. Everyone not only does it their own way, they spend a good deal of energy telling everyone else (including college coaches) they don't know what they are doing.

• Recently, I've seen very competitive junior teams cheat by placing their libero wherever she is needed in passing until the second referee, usually another club coach, catches the overlap. The message these programs are sending to their players is that okay to break the rules if you can get away with it. When a junior coach does this it also makes college coaches wonder if the information the club is using to promote their players such as vertical jump statistics and ACT scores is accurate, or if there are exaggerations on the website as well.

• When Title IX was first enacted most coaches understood, along with trying to win, we had a responsibility to create opportunities for women, both on the court and our staffs. This resulted in conferences making it a priority to hire female coaches. The former Pac-10 and the Big Ten conferences played leadership roles in promoting this mission.

Money has become more important than mission. A few years ago, the Pac-10 did not have one female head volleyball coach. (With the addition of Colorado and Utah to form the Pac-12 they gained two female head coaches.) Recently Big Ten teams have twice hired completely male staffs, while noting that a volunteer coach and the person who works with the team strength program are females.

The coaches and athletic directors making these decisions are good people working hard to put their programs in the best position to win. Most coaches in women's sports would be horrified if the NCAA moved to cut the number of scholarships available in the women's sport they coach, and they would make their argument based on the principles, goals and spirit of Title IX.

Imagine a public school district building as a school that had the resources to provide a great education to minority students but then hired only white teachers, justifying the decision because there would be volunteer minority teacher-aides and minorites working in the cafeteria, \while noting "we couldn't find qualified minority candidates."

• One of the challenges for NCAA Division I volleyball is as the budgets and salaries continue to grow, the focus has become protecting the gains in support that women's volleyball has received instead of becoming accountable for income generation. If coaches at major Division I programs want the benefits they are reaping in higher salaries, perhaps athletic directors should hold them accountable for specific attendance goals and season ticket sales. No business (and volleyball coaches want to be paid like successful business people) can afford to have a staff of four to five full-time employees managing only twelve to fourteen players without expecting that same staff to have a plan for generating more attendance and income.

TERRY PETTIT

THE LAST MINTONETTE
CLUB IN AMERICA

I first heard there was an active Mintonette Club on the East Coast in the 1970s. At the time I considered the information highly improbable, similar to the reports of ivory-billed woodpeckers living in the sweet gum forests of eastern Arkansas after the bird had not been seen in more than thirty years. If there were such a club, then surely it was part of a historical reenactment in the same way American wags dress up in Civil War costumes, fire muskets, and somehow have great fun in simulating the bloodiest battles in American history.

As it turns out, there was at least one pair of ivory-billed woodpeckers still alive in America. In 2004, David Luneau, a Georgia Tech graduate and a professor at the University of Arkansas-Little Rock, identified and filmed *"The Lord God Bird"* believed to have been extinct since 1944 (two years after Mintonette inventor William G. Morgan's death) in the swampy Big Woods area of eastern Arkansas. Ornithologists, volleyball coaches, doubters, and other woodpeckers can view it for themselves at: http://www.youtube.com/watch?v=q8SvfXvFZbE.

Unlike ivory-bills, I had not thought much about Mintonette for forty years, until a retired Canadian Olympic volleyball coach mentioned it to me at a brewpub in Fort Collins, Colorado. We were finishing a round of Cutthroat Porters in Old Town, when he asked me if I was familiar with the word "*Mintonette*."

"Of course," I said, "Mintonette is the name William Morgan gave to the game he invented in 1896, a game designed to provide exercise in moderation for men and women who no longer had the inclination to play basketball or ride horses."

"Two years later the name was changed to volleyball because some of Morgan's friends thought the name was too feminine," he responded. "What would you think," my Canadian friend continued, "If I told you there is a Mintonette Club in upstate New York that has been in existence for close to a hundred years?"

"I wouldn't believe it," I replied, "But if there was one, I would want to know how I could find it, and how it has avoided tweets, YouTube, and Pinterest."

Last winter, I found myself boarding the Amtrak Adirondack for a journey north toward a destination near the Canadian border. I carried a small backpack, a laptop, and a recently-purchased Panasonic Lumix camera in the unlikely event if I actually found the Mintonette Club, I could take photographs for proof. I was however, more prepared to discover I had been sent on an elaborate goose chase by a practical joker who would be telling this story to colleagues in pubs throughout Canada for years to come.

When I departed the train in Woods Falls, New York (this is not the real name of the town for reasons you will soon understand), I went to a building on *Rue Principale* which had been a former YMCA. It was a weathered, red brick building that had a cornerstone dated 1922. Inside it housed a balcony running track (sixteen laps to a mile). I climbed a metal circular staircase in the corner and looked down onto what appeared to be a very small volleyball court.

Within a few minutes, several men and women came into the gymnasium where they proceeded to set up what appeared to be badminton net made out of hemp. I began a slow jog on the balcony track so as to not appear to be watching. No one looked up, probably because a slow jog seems very appropriate for someone of my age and fitness.

The top of the net was about six and one-half feet high. The ball the players volleyed back and forth was slightly larger than a soccer ball with a leather skin sewn together by heavy stitching. The teams began playing, seven on a side, with what appeared to be a 3-1-3 defensive system. Each team had an extra player who rotated in following a side-out.

Everyone, both men and women, wore a white t-shirt with barely readable script that said, "*Woods Falls Mintonette Club — 1913.*" The game they played allowed three contacts on a side but a teammate was allowed to "help" a player's serve over the net if the ball was going to fall short.

The teams played two games of twenty-five minutes each, with everyone serving three balls before rotating. The match seemed more friendly than competitive, with both sides trying to keep the ball in play for as long as possible while shouting encouragement to their opponents. In one rally alone I counted twenty-seven contacts before the ball fell to the floor, with both sides celebrating the length of the point. The players shouted encouragement with every contact of the ball. A pack of beagles on the hunt could not have been happier.

And then, after fifty minutes everything stopped, the players joined hands in a circle at the center of the gym where they bowed their heads for several seconds, and then in astonishingly melodic voices sang "*Mintonette! Mintonette! Mintonette!*" before hugging each other like Quakers and leaving for separate locker rooms that were off limits to all but club members.

About a half-hour later the club secretary, who had been on the court earlier, joined me on a park bench across the street from the club. She agreed to meet with me if I promised to withhold her name from this story. She told me her mother, father, and grandparents on each side had been members of the Mintonette Club, and as far as she knew, her great grandparents as well. Out of respect for the club, she asked me not to share photographs or identify the community where the last Mintonette Club in America resided.

"The club has endured every possible challenge for the past ninety-seven years; from floods, to bankruptcy, to the challenge of making our own Mintonette balls, to our sons and daughters wanting to play *Call of Duty: Modern Warfare* instead of Mintonette," she said, "But I'm not sure we can survive the curiosity of strangers. Mintonette is more a game of collaboration than what most Americans are familiar with and I don't think outsiders would understand the hold that the game has on us."

As she spoke I kept thinking I've seen this woman before, her posture, her combination of confidence wrapped in modesty, but before I could respond, she said, "Thank you for understanding," while waving good-bye, walking across the street with a slightly out-of-round Mintonette ball cradled beneath her arm, hoping a stranger might comply with her wishes.

I have done my best to both honor her request and describe a game that has endured, despite competing with a culture which does not foster informal, spontaneous play where there is no clear-cut winner and loser. It is even harder to imagine a game whose participants are shyer than "The Lord God Birds" that disappeared from this country for most of the twentieth century.

LOOKING FOR GHOSTS

Horseteeth Ringen. The phrase sounds like a Russian greeting in translation or perhaps a salute before tossing down a shot of whiskey at an Irish racetrack. It isn't either; it was a boy's name.

When I was a kid in Northwest Indiana my father stopped the car across from a vacant lot near the Shell station on the north side of town. "That," he said, "Used to be Brown's Field where we played pickup baseball when I was growing up. Horseteeth Ringen hit a home run here one day, touched first, second, and third, and then when he touched home plate, collapsed and died of a heart attack."

I was mortified. A little bit because the thought of a twelve-year-old kid having a heart attack was frightening, but mostly because this poor kid, who could be me, had the nickname "Horseteeth." Even with the backlash against political correctness this couldn't happen today.

But nicknames were still around in the 1950s and 1960s. There was a kid who played basketball at my college who was called "The Kosiosko County Jumping Jack." My two favorite nicknames are both from baseball, first for one of the greatest first basemen of all time, Stan "the Man" Musial, and second, a pun on Musial's nickname given to a relief pitcher named Don Stanhouse whose combination of Harpo Marx hair and primal screams led an ESPN wag to give him the nickname, "Stan the Man Unusual."

Today most nicknames are the first letters of a teammate's first and second names: K.D., C.J., T.K., or hybrids of the first name with a couple of letters tacked on: Kimmer, Jimmer, and Emster. I wonder if in the South, "Bigun" is still popular. Horseteeth, Badfeet, Enormous Head, Slowtwitch, and Smelly would be snipped off in the first encounter with organized sport, which for most kids is about three.

Some of you are probably wondering if the story about Horseteeth is true. It is, but because it took place in the 1930s you are going to have to take my word for it. If it happened after 1994 you could look it up. Horseteeth would likely be on Facebook or MySpace and possibly have an account with Friendster, LinkedIn, Twitter, or Classmates.com. If Horseteeth's last name was Swenson you could possibly find him on Lunar Storm, a networking site in Sweden, and if he had a true disability, not just bad teeth, you might find him on Disaboom, a network for people with multiple sclerosis, cerebral palsy, and other health issues.

But of course Horseteeth died before any of this existed. Horseteeth died before television and Pez dispensers. If he collapsed after hitting a home run in 1995 you could Google his name, search for him on Pipl.com, and chances are you would find an archived news story about an unfortunate kid who collapsed in a field in Crown Point, Indiana, with an undetected heart defect, while playing an unauthorized game of baseball next to a Pennsylvania Railroad roadbed where the tracks had been ripped up thirty years ago.

She would be fifty-six years old now; five foot ten inches tall, although if she were still wearing the Afro she had when I first met her in 1974, her personality, her presence, and her hair would make her seem much taller. Her most distinguishing characteristic besides her skin color would be the fact that she was left-handed.

Carolyn Hawkins was from Henderson, North Carolina, nineteen miles and forty-five minutes north of Louisburg College, one of the oldest two-year colleges in the United States. Louisburg College was chartered in 1787, held its first classes in 1805, and became Louisburg Female Academy in 1815.

Carolyn and I both arrived in Louisburg in the fall of 197. She was one of the first female athletes to be recruited on an athletic scholarship, while I was hired to teach English and coach men's golf and tennis. Neither of us was prepared to be a part of the first women's volleyball team Louisburg College fielded and both of us assumed our roles, mine as coach and Carolyn's as player, by happenstance.

Carolyn was recruited to play on Louisburg's first women's basketball team by the head coach, Sam White, a confirmed bachelor who had spent most of his life coaching baseball at multiple levels in small towns throughout the South. I became the volleyball coach one week before practice began when the president of the college overheard a conversation at a dinner party that I had played for a men's team in Chicago.

Both of us assumed our roles because we were asked. Carolyn was encouraged to try out by her high school basketball teammate, Debbie Tyson, who was also recruited to play basketball at Louisburg, and who would later go on to become the head volleyball coach at the University of Virginia. I said yes to the president when asked, although I thought he was talking about a men's team. I was no more aware of the fact that Title IX legislation had been passed the year before, providing opportunity for women in sports, than I was that woods and ponds north of the college were home to copperheads, water moccasins, abandoned tobacco barns, and large mouth bass bigger than possums.

Carolyn had two nicknames: "Hawk" and "Turkey." The first was an abbreviation of her last name but also conveyed the change in alertness that came over her in competition. The second was a high school nickname which I assumed referred to her ability to become the center of good-natured kidding about her tendency to be oblivious to whatever was happening whenever she was not in competition.

On a team of fifteen players, none of who had ever played organized volleyball, her number was eighteen, which was only possible because we made our own uniforms from shirts and cloth bought in Raleigh. The numbers were sewn on by a lady who was friend of Dr. Ruth Cook, who served as Louisburg College's first senior women's administrator, and who watched women's basketball and volleyball competitions from a lawn chair perched on a stage in the gymnasium.

Because we ran a 4-2 with the setter positioned at the net in the middle of the court, Carolyn was both a left side and right side attacker, although using those terms would indicate more tactical preparedness than was actually the case. She was the first player in the history of Louisburg volleyball to attack the ball, and by the end of her sophomore season was probably the second-best attacker in a state that has as many NCAA Division I schools as any in the country.

Her development as spiker allowed her to earn a full volleyball scholarship to the University of North Carolina at Chapel Hill when she graduated from Louisburg with her junior college degree. She may have been the first black female athlete to play volleyball for North Carolina, which was located fifty-five miles and an hour-and-a-half from Louisburg depending upon which two-lane roads you took, and how many men with hats on were driving below the 50 miles per hour speed limit.

She was not the first black athlete. Phil Ford was running the famed four corners offense for Dean Smith and Tar Heel basketball. Local rival North Carolina State had recently won its first national championship with David Thompsen, whose vertical jump challenged the laws of physics. Duke had not yet become "Duke." The Atlantic Coast Conference was becoming the best men's basketball conference in the country. Women's volleyball, like women's sports in general, was like a small amusement park ride on the edge of the state fair.

If Chapel Hill seemed like a charming, progressive college town that might appear on the cover of the *Saturday Evening Post* to most people, it must have been a culture shock to someone raised in Henderson, North Carolina, via Louisburg College. Small towns in the Piedmont were in a parallel universe waffling between 1775 and 1955.

Farmers still played marbles at near dusk in Rocky Mount, North Carolina. The owner of a small breakfast café, which was my first restaurant meal in Louisburg, talked about "darkies" while he was cooking sausage on the grill. Public sanitation did not include the black neighborhood on the other side of the river. White folks vacationed and golfed at Nags Head or drove south to Myrtle Beach. Black folks fished with worms in the Tar River.

Nineteen seventy-five marked the second year for integration at the high schools. Four drugstores were located at the same intersection on the square in a town of 2,000 people. The movie theater had been closed for several years. Entertainment outside of high school sports was still segregated. People rooted for "State" or "Carolina" for different reasons: white people because they were alums, black people because of David Thompson, Charlie Scott, and Phil Ford.

The campus that Carolyn moved to was bivouacked in the twentieth century. Chapel Hill was actively recruiting black athletes to compete with North Carolina State. The Carolina Coffee shop on Franklin Street welcomed blacks as did the men's store across the street, which provided the men's basketball staff and players with as deep a discount as you can get on the dress suits players wore when they traveled. (On most college campuses in the 1970s, discrimination was not primarily black and white, but football and men's basketball on one plane and every other sport on another. To some degree this continues at many major institutions.)

Nineteen seventy-six was Carolyn's first year at North Carolina and my last year at Louisburg before moving to the University of Nebraska. We competed against each other that fall with Louisburg winning in straight sets, and Carolyn playing well for the Tar Heels. After the match she was more "Turkey" than "Hawk," mingling with her former teammates, laughing while being both the center of attention and affection.

I could tell she missed the intimacy of Louisburg, but I was also reassured because her head coach at North Carolina, Beth Miller, was a very caring coach who would provide all the support Carolyn needed to succeed in an opportunity that none of us could have dreamed of two years before. Beth told me while Carolyn faced the challenges any student does from moving to a major university from a small liberal arts two-year college, she was confident Carolyn would ultimately succeed and graduate with a degree from one of the most prestigious schools in the country. And she did.

She played her senior year but then I lost track of her, partly because I was consumed with my own challenges at my new coaching position at Nebraska and partly because there was no Internet, no cell phones, no texting, no Twitter, no Facebook. I would run into some of her former teammates who entered the coaching profession at clinics and conventions, and following hugs and embraces our first interaction almost always was, "Have you seen Carolyn? Do you know where she is?" And then we would retell stories about how we could get her to perform at a higher level in practice if we had someone come in and pretend to video tape her for the Raleigh evening news.

In the early 1980s one of my best friends, Terry Davis, a former basketball and volleyball coach at Louisburg High School, told me he thought he saw her walking down the street in Greensboro, North Carolina, but by the time he double tracked she was gone.

There were reports, with no attribution, that she had joined the military, and then for a year or two there was rumor she had died, either in an accident or perhaps in military service. With the advent of the Internet, several of us have tried to find her. Her family is gone from Henderson. I phoned the administrative offices at Louisburg College and they did not have any records indicating that she ever attended the school. I was so dumfounded I couldn't speak.

Beth Miller lost track of Carolyn as well. There are more than forty Carolyn Hawkins listed on LinkedIn living in North Carolina. There are hundreds on Facebook, but none of the images have her countenance or smile. Of course she could be married with a different name. She could be living in Europe. Pipl.com does not list any death records that would correspond to her age, but she could be deceased.

I've explored all the best people search engines: Google, 123people, Spock, and Spokeo. There are pay sites which are probably more thorough but I have been hesitant to use those resources for a couple of reasons. After two years of searching for a former high school teammate, I finally found a phone number and address and there was a 99 percent chance that it was him. His relatives all matched. The age matched. Everything said it was him. But I hesitated. Why?

Something in me said that perhaps he didn't want to be found. He hadn't checked in at his high school or college websites. He hadn't contacted any of our mutual friends. He or anyone from his family hadn't been seen at class reunions in more than thirty years. Two years ago I called someone I thought for sure was him based on a picture on Facebook. Same bone structure. Same interests. Same age. The gentleman laughed and said he understood my passion to find my friend. But it wasn't him. That is one reason. And the other reason . . . perhaps she is gone and as long as I don't know for sure there is hope.

So why do I do this? Am I looking for someone from my past or am I looking for myself in my past. With a former player it's different. Even when they are fifty-six, it is like looking for a lost child. There is a sense that I should have made more of an effort; I should have made sure that she was doing okay. I should have been there when she enlisted, got married, or disappeared.

To some degree Carolyn Hawkins represents the first generation of young women who had the opportunity to compete. They played before there were accurate statistics or records. They played before there were media guides or YouTube. For the most part, their pictures are not in trophy cases and they are either too busy to attend or not invited to reunions. They are becoming ghosts, but they still live in their coach's mind. If I saw her today coming around the corner, if by chance I am lucky enough to find out that she is alive, healthy and doing well, this is what I would say:

"Hawk, how are we doing?"

Girl's volleyball team: FRONT ROW — J. Siegner, J. Tant, S. Creech, D. Duke, M. Mayes, D. Tyson, L. Capps, M. Person. SECOND ROW — Mrs. Petit, M. Clark, C. Tant, C. Hawkins, D. Rogers, S. Howell, E. Pernell, S. Credle, Mr. Pettit.

THE BEAUTIFUL GAME

In 1980 one of the top NCAA Division I volleyball recruits in the Midwest was Erin Dean, a five foot nine outside hitter from Kansas City. If she had been a baseball player she would have been known as a "five-tool player." She was an exceptional attacker, passer, defender, server, and ball handler. Her blocking, while not as strong as her other skills, was more than adequate, and her alertness, hand-eye coordination, arm-speed, and competitiveness made her an exceptional all-around player.

If Erin were a high school senior today there is a very good chance she would not choose to play collegiate volleyball. Specialization has led to an increasing emphasis on size so if Erin wanted to play for a Division I team today, she would most likely have the option of being a libero or a back row specialist. The thought of not being on the court at all times might lead her to choose basketball, soccer, softball, or another team sport.

The addition of the libero, unlimited entries by a player, and most recently, the decision by the volleyball rules committee to allow fifteen substitutions has chipped away at the concept of the all-around player. Women's collegiate volleyball is becoming a platoon game, where on many teams the only constants are the setter and the libero.

Front row players specialize in attacking and blocking; back row defenders specialize in passing, ball handling, defending, and pursuit. It is not too difficult to imagine sometime in the near future we may even eliminate the concept of rotating. The question is have we created a better game?

There are several things which make volleyball a unique sport, but the one factor that really separates it from other team sports is the concept of rotating positions. To appreciate just how remarkable that is, imagine if you rotated positions in baseball. After the first inning, the pitcher would move behind the plate, the catcher would move to first base, the first baseman to second, the second baseman to third, etc.

Volleyball is different than other team sports in that the team on the attack can choose which player has to play the ball on the opposite side of the net. In basketball we can't force the opponent's weakest defender to guard our best shooter, but in volleyball we *can* direct the attack to a specific backcourt defender. Prior to substitution rule changes in recent years, there was a tremendous advantage when the opposing coach was forced to keep a strong net player with modest ball handling skills in the match. If the coach wanted her to play in the front row he couldn't substitute for her in the back row if she already had three entries. Size was only important if the player also had developed at least some level of proficiency in all-around skills.

Because of almost unlimited substitutions, size has become exponentially more important than technical skills. The tallest players are, for the most part, recruited to the power conferences. If a coach has a choice between a six foot five middle blocker with weak ball handling skills or a six foot middle blocker with tremendous all-around skills, the nod goes to the bigger net player. With fifteen subs, a libero, and a bench filled with great back row players, there is no downside to recruiting the bigger but less complete player.

Some coaches believe more substitutions and specialization create a more level playing field. It doesn't. While specializing with front row and back row players at every position helps a mediocre program get better, it significantly helps the programs with the most talent (size) because they are more likely to have deeper benches.

Collegiate volleyball coaches gave up the opportunity to tactically exploit taller players when the three-entry rule was removed. Fifteen substitutions make that even easier, and over time more substitutions will place even more emphasis on recruiting and less on training.

The decision by the rules committee to move to fifteen substitutions is supposedly motivated by creating more opportunity. If that is the case, I believe it is misguided. If you want to create more opportunity for women then increase the number of scholarships, which has a direct impact on how many young women choose to play a sport. Women's soccer has the highest number of scholarships to offer (fourteen) and yet it has very strict rules on substitutions which limit the number of entries into a half. That has not kept young women from flocking to club soccer teams in search of scholarships.

For NCAA Division II, III, or NAIA coaches who believe more scholarships would mean less talent at their institutions, ask yourself this question: if Division I only had six scholarships instead of twelve, would your roster in five years be more talented or less talented? For a year or two you would benefit, but over time the more scholarship opportunities offered the more women enter the game, the stronger the talent at all levels.

Sometimes I think we get lucky when we first develop a sport. The distance from the mound to the plate in baseball seems as perfect as the golden mean. If the mound were any closer to the plate or any further from the plate it would dramatically change the game. If the distance between the bases changed, we wouldn't have the close calls that make baseball exciting for some of us.

The thing that makes volleyball such a beautiful game is its rhythm. The addition of the libero doesn't destroy that rhythm because of its seamless substitution, while it also allows for the extraordinary, shorter athlete who is choosing to play shortstop in softball or point guard in basketball to have the opportunity in volleyball.

With fifteen substitutions, however, we are moving further away from a game where every player has to learn every skill to something approaching an off-Broadway play, where the lead actors change with every scene. There will be fewer upsets, less emphasis on training all-around fundamentals, even more emphasis on size and a fundamental misunderstanding about how opportunity is created. Changing the rules of the game to create more part-time players does not create opportunity; funding the recruitment and training of people from diverse backgrounds to play the game creates opportunity.

Having said that, fifteen substitutions may not seem dramatic, even to the majority of coaches who prefer twelve or fewer substitutions because for thirty years we have been chipping away at a game that most of us can't remember. The best way to create opportunity is not by making the game less attractive but by giving more people the opportunity to play the beautiful game.

DON'T MISTAKE COLLABORATION
FOR WEAKNESS

During my second year as head coach of the University of Nebraska women's volleyball team, my coaching career almost came to an abrupt end. Two faculty members told me my assistant coach was undermining my leadership and was trying to persuade the senior women's administrator to replace me with himself as the head coach.

At first I ignored the information, but when the SWA showed up at the end of the last practice before the NCAA Regional Championship and handed the players "Head Coach Evaluation" forms, I knew the rumors were true. My wife and I had a one-year-old daughter and on a salary of $12,000 a year, we hadn't been able to put much into savings. If I lost my job, I would not only be unemployed, but quite likely would never coach again.

At that moment one of the most remarkable things during my career occurred because of the courage of the team captain. After she read the evaluation and sensed what the intent was, she gathered the forms from her teammates and handed them back to the SWA while stating, "This is not appropriate."

This was also interesting because I don't think the team captain was thrilled about some of the decisions I had made, nor was she making a statement about the potential she saw in me as a head coach. She did it because she thought the undermining of a head coach was inherently wrong. Her decision was based on values.

After talking with a coaching friend who was much more experienced than I was, I confronted the SWA about the disloyalty and she supported my decision to fire the assistant coach. (In my mind it might have been just as appropriate if she, the SWA, had fired herself as well.) Strangely enough, the team rallied, and came together to win Nebraska's first regional championship, defeating a very strong Southwest Missouri State squad coached by hall of fame coach, Linda Dollar.

With the final point, the same SWA who wanted to fire me two weeks before grabbed the microphone and broadcasted how proud she was that the University of Nebraska volleyball program would represent the region in the AIAW National Championship at the University of Alabama.

I have become aware of the story of an assistant coach trying to subvert the leadership of a head coach all too frequently in recent years. A few years ago one of my former players who had entered the coaching profession told me of another assistant coach who was trying to manipulate a prominent and highly-successful head coach into retirement.

Eventually she shared what she knew with the head coach and after he confirmed her observations he called and asked me for my opinion. Was it possible to reform someone who had violated his trust? I told him the same thing that had been told to me thirty years before when I faced the same decision.

He needed to fire the assistant coach immediately. If someone isn't working hard enough, or needs to learn to communicate more effectively, or needs to take more ownership in the tasks they have been assigned, there still may be potential for that person to develop. But if someone violates your trust, which is the most important contract in a coaching relationship, the issue is not skills development but character. Keeping a person on your staff who cannot be trusted not only puts you and your program in jeopardy, it doesn't give that person the best opportunity to understand how serious their mistake was and the chance to consider adjusting their values before they take their next position.

Four years ago a similar situation happened again. A junior college coach who had been hired to take over a foundering NCAA Division I volleyball program hired a peer to become her first assistant, and hired his assistant coach to be her second assistant. Halfway through their first season, the first assistant asked to meet with the director of athletics where he offered the opinion that he believed he should switch positions with the head coach because he knew significantly more about volleyball than she did. The director of athletics fired him on the spot.

Sometimes assistant coaches can perceive a head coach's eagerness to collaborate with them as a sign of weakness. There may be areas of coaching where an assistant coach believes she has a stronger skill-set than the head coach, but it would be a mistake to believe that a skill-set, knowledge, or the perceived vulnerability of the head coach is more important than embracing and modeling the behaviors and values that an educational institution aspires to.

Assistant coaches can welcome the opportunity to take ownership of any element of training, recruiting, or team building that is offered by a head coach, but they should not interpret such empowerment as an opportunity to promote themselves into a position of power. They are more likely to be seen as a fool by the people they are hoping to lead, and they will be convincing the administrators who make such decisions that the assistant coach has a fundamental misunderstanding of leadership by placing his ego ahead of integrity and trust.

I survived my situation because of the mentoring of a more-experienced coach and the leadership of a twenty-one-year-old player. While I would not wish that dilemma on any head coach, it also gave a young woman the opportunity to make a value-based decision which would become a pattern in her life as a mother, educator, and a high school coach.

TERRY PETTIT

THE SEVEN HABITS
AND PSYCHIC KAY

Stephen Covey, the American educator, author, and motivational speaker died in the summer of 2012 at the age of seventy-nine. His most famous book, *The Seven Habits of Highly Effective People,* has sold more than twenty-five million copies in thirty-eight languages since its first publication. One of Covey's most interesting insights is that the most vulnerable organizations are the ones that are entrenched in success.

To my knowledge, Covey never had coffee with Psychic Kay, a palm reader who lived and practiced mental telepathy in a pink and white house at the edge of Fort Collins, Colorado, until she was evicted by her landlord. Psychic Kay (aka Kathy Adams) either wasn't aware of the marketing implications of what she was saying or had a tremendous sense of humor when she commented about losing her lease in the Coloradoan and said, *"I didn't see it coming."*

In their own way, both Covey and Kay spent their adult lives focused on different aspects of the same conundrum: human behavior. Covey died of injuries from a bicycle accident he sustained three months before his death. His personal life was consistent with his philosophy of living life by taking risks. Kay was murdered by her common law husband as she was planning to flee from his abuse. Her intuition gave her a plan of action but it did not arrive in time to save her.

Both Covey and Kay speak to issues that should be of interest to high school and collegiate coaches. Covey warns us that coaches who have been "entrenched" in success may be the most stubborn about acting on necessary adaptations. Kay warns us that we can be undone by both what we know and what we don't know.

With success comes hubris: we start to believe there is a predictable continuum to our coaching legacy. We believe the most important ingredient to our success is our insight and experience. We start taking fewer risks. We delegate without empowering. We run the same drills with the same key words, without spending any energy to put ourselves in the uncomfortable situations which are necessary for growth. Our brain becomes a media guide.

We can be undone by what we know: the graduation of primary passers can be more devastating to a team than the loss of dominant attackers. Chemistry in volleyball is directly related to consistent passing. We know this but we never fail to recruit a six foot three project over a five foot eleven all-around ball handler.

The return of several starters from a championship team does not guarantee repeated success. Players sometimes do not understand *why* they were successful. Because players' expectations change they may or may not embrace new roles. History is the path we took to win the conference championship last year. Even when we have the same people on the team, the journey is different with another season. Trust has to be rebuilt before we can summit.

Coaches are both teachers and performers. How a head coach handles increased expectations, and how she handles disappointing losses or unexpected challenges is as least as important as whether or not players respond and embrace the adjustments they are being asked to make. Unless a head coach is very alert it is easy for anxiety to replace hope as a base position.

We can be undone by our own behaviors: Despite vowing to become the strongest-serving team in the conference, we don't act on that decision by working on technical serving and implementing competitive serving drills in every practice. Later in the season we are faced with trying to defeat a team that is bigger and more athletic than we are. Our lack of discipline as coaches prevents us from taking charge of the one element of the game (serving) which would allow us to be competitive.

In the second half of the season we spend the majority of our time in opponent preparation as opposed to refining and leveraging our strengths. Practice feels more like hanging on than moving toward anything extraordinary.

We can also be undone by what we don't know: the death of a teammate, the pain and fatigue of dealing with a scandal associated with the athletic department, the questionable health of a potentially dominant player, the lack of focus by an experienced setter, the difference between the pressure of winning and defending expectations, the possibility that we have been playing the wrong person in the wrong position, these and a thousand other frogs perch at the edge of a successful season.

There is also this insight that experienced coaches use to assuage the amygdale: even if I do everything right, play the right people, get flu shots in September, communicate in the most positive and effective way, spend hours on developing systems that leverage our strengths, and more hours in individual training so that we can implement a tactical game plan, *it is still their team. Their decisions will determine whether or not we become something special.*

Despite the noise that accompanies these challenges, sixty-five teams have been selected to play in the NCAA Division I volleyball tournament, but the seeding won't work out for some of them, and so there may be a head coach who didn't anticipate playing a highly-ranked first-round opponent in the Wooden Center in Los Angeles. When the sports information director asks her for a quote on the draw and tournament field, she may recall something she read from a palm reader in Colorado and reply, *"I didn't see it coming."*

TERRY PETTIT

HOW EXTRAORDINARY COACHING
IMITATES A BASKETBALL MOVIE

My favorite scene in the 1986 movie *Hoosiers* is when head coach Norman Dale, played by Gene Hackman, greets his new team for the first time while holding a whistle:

"Huddle up. My name is Norman Dale and I coached college ball for ten years, but it has been twelve years since I blew this, so I'm going to learn as much from you as you learn from me."

When Norman Dale first meets the Hickory Huskers in a small-town gymnasium in 1954, the Huskers are anything but whole. The team's best player, Jimmy Chitwood, has chosen not to play on the team following the death of the previous head coach. Dale has just fired the assistant coach, and before the huddle breaks, two of the team's remaining eight players quit the team. With their departure Dale observes, "It's going to be a lonely bench with only seven players," before the shortest team member corrects him by telling him that he really only has six players, because the speaker "ain't no good," and he is really just the equipment manager. Yikes!

The script for *Hoosiers* was inspired by a legendary story in Indiana high school basketball. In 1954 the small town of Milan won the all-class state championship, defeating a much larger school with a storied history, the Muncie Central Bearcats, in the championship game played in front of 15,000-plus fans in Hinkle Fieldhouse on the campus of

Butler University. The game ended when Milan's star player, Bobby Plump, who would go on to play for Butler, dribbles the ball for twelve seconds until he fires a jump shot from the top of the key, resulting in a swish that still reverberates in gymnasiums and backyard baskets throughout the state.

There are several reasons this scene and the *Hoosiers* story has such resonance with me. Of all the things I miss in coaching, the opportunity to call a team to attention with the phrase "huddle up" is at the top of my list. For me, a huddle was more than just the chance to share information with a team. It was the opportunity to reaffirm, or in today's terminology, reboot our commitment to each other and our sense of purpose. A huddle in competition was even better; nostrils flared, eyes dilated, with everyone breathing the inherent hope living in the DNA of a huddle during a big match, was as good as coaching got for me.

While the movie loosely parallels Milan's journey to the state championship, basketball in itself is not what makes the movie great. The movie has several story lines, all of them involving second chances. Chitwood, Hickory's best player has the chance to redeem himself when he rejoins the team. Wilbur "Shooter" Flatch, played by Dennis Hopper, a former Hickory player and father to one of the current players, has the chance to become more than the town drunk when Dale asks him to become an assistant coach. Barbara Hershey plays Myra Fleener, a high school English teacher whose sex appeal ranges from "disinterested" to "why bother," and whose mission in life appears to be to keep Chitwood from rejoining the high school team so he can focus on academics and get a scholarship to Wabash College.

But it's Hackman's portrayal of a flawed coach, who has to come to terms with his past, his limitations, and his willingness to be open to a different kind of leadership that elevates *Hoosiers* beyond a pleasant basketball fairytale to a movie that was nominated for two Oscars, and is considered perhaps the best sports movie of all time.

There is a reason Dale hasn't coached in twelve years and it isn't a lack of knowledge or past on-court success. In a scene where Dale is going for a walk with Fleener on her mother's farm, Fleener confronts Dale with his past.

Fleener begins, "Norman Dale coach of the Ithaca Warriors has been suspended . . ." but before she can continue, Dale interrupts: "I can't really explain that . . . It's been a number of years and it still kind of goes around in my head. I slow it down . . . sometimes I think I can stop my fist from hitting that boy's jaw. In one second everything I worked for was just all finished."

So there it is. Dale in his mid-fifties is not just flawed when the movie begins; he is a broken man, blackballed, and out of coaching, until he accepts the opportunity to coach in the smallest of high school communities, one in which the basketball team's lack of success creates a "last chance" offering for both the head coach and several of the characters in the movie.

This is where *Hoosiers* departs from the Milan legend and becomes a more complex, and to everyone outside Milan, Indiana, a more interesting story. Hackman, as an actor, has one of most important qualities in an extraordinary coach: preparation. How many times have you watched a movie where you had some familiarity with the events or the characters portrayed and you came away thinking that the actors didn't get it quite right?

Despite all of his practice with teaching pros and the overall entertainment of the movie *Tin Cup*, Kevin Costner's posture and the tempo of his golf swing never convinces me he has ever had to make a par with ten bucks on the line. But Hackman has it all right. His goal as an actor, as he once said in an interview, is not to appear natural but real. And when he teaches the Huskers how to pass a basketball by "popping the ball," I can smell the leather as he rotates his wrists.

As *Hoosiers* evolves, Dale, through Hackman, does the three things which are the lifeblood of extraordinary coaching: he recruits, he requires, and he relates. When the Huskers are learning to pass the ball, Dale speaks over the drill and recruits to his philosophy when he says, "Let's be real clear about what we're after here . . . the five players on the floor function as one single unit . . . team, team, team . . . no one more important than the other."

(Sometimes high school coaches believe they don't recruit; but they do. The most consistent high school programs have the best athletes in the school involved in their sport. Both high school and college coaches know their livelihood also depends upon their ability to recruit team members to embrace their roles, and commit to behaviors which allow the team to have the best chance for success. In every interaction, every behavior, every organized practice plan or communication with a team, a head coach is recruiting players, parents, administrators, and a community to a vision of what the head coach believes is possible.)

Coaches recognize the importance of goals but sometimes don't value importance of purpose or confuse it with the former. Goals are measurable; purpose is not. In the scene before the final game in the regional championship Dale speaks to the difference when he addresses his team before leaving the locker room:

"Forget about the crowds, the size of the school, their fancy uniforms, and remember what got you here. Focus on the fundamentals that we've gone over time and time again. And most important don't get caught up thinking about winning or losing this game. If you put your effort and concentration into playing to your potential, to be the best that you can be; I don't care what the scoreboard says at the end of the game, in my book we are going to be winners."

Purpose is based on values. Effort, concentration, focus, and integrity are values that can't be measured, but their existence is what determines the culture of a team. (I have always believed when high school athletes make decisions about what schools they were going to consider attending in college, they did so by comparing their options with their own personal goals. But after visiting the three or four schools they had culled their list down to, their final decision is based on their intuitive sense of the culture they discovered with a college coaching staff, team, or institution.)

Requiring comes easy for Dale, as it is for many coaches. Transactional communication with players is where teaching often begins. This was particularly true in the 1950s when trust came with authority. If the coach said to have your palms up on defense, there wasn't a discussion. When we first teach kids to pass a volleyball, we ask them to place one hand in the other and extend a platform from the shoulders. Placing one hand on the opposite elbow is not an option. Cracking the platform at the elbows in not an option.

Dale understands that coaching is about changing behaviors. The results on the scoreboard only change as a result of changing behaviors in how we practice, how we prepare, and with the quality of our preparation. He demands non-negotiable behaviors which allow his team to be efficient in their preparation and execution: "Four passes before every shot."

Requiring is the same as directing, and it can be an effective form of leadership. When a coach has an inexperienced setter in high school competition, it may be appropriate for the coach to direct a setter on where and to whom to set the ball in each rotation if it gives the team the best chance to side-out. Directing is also appropriate in crisis. If there is a fire in the building it helps to have someone telling us the safest route to exit. But directing has its limitations as a player gains skills and experience.

This is the challenge for Dale. When the movie begins he is only capable of transactional (directed) leadership, and he has some success because the Huskers are in crisis. He teaches them how to dribble, how to maintain posture on defense, how block-out, how to set screens, how to give great effort. But directed leadership may not be successful when the tempo of the game against a talented opponent requires adjustments by the players on the floor.

Let me give you an example. Earlier I said if we had an inexperienced setter it might be helpful to her to recognize situations and make the most effective calls when siding out. This is leadership directed by a coaching staff. What we hope to grow into is "coached leadership" and eventually "collaborative leadership." Coached leadership is when we teach a setter how to execute a game plan by the setter recognizing which decisions are going to be the most successful in specific situations.

Several years ago, we were playing one of Don Shaw's great Stanford teams and the Cardinal had the strongest net player in college volleyball in Kerri Walsh. We would be limited in influencing whether or not Stanford set Walsh who was a right side attacker, but through our setter's decision making we could limit Walsh's impact as a blocker on our left side attackers.

Our setter, Fiona Nepo, was coached to run our quick attackers at Walsh (31s) only if she planned on setting the ball in the opposite direction. If she wanted to set our quick attackers she needed to call for a tight or wide slide. In Stanford's first rotation where Walsh stayed at left front after serve receive, the opposite would be true. Fiona would respond by setting 31s to our quick attacker, running away from Walsh, or setting "go" sets to our left side attackers.

Fiona was "coached" into making the most effective decisions based on a strategy as opposed to the coaching staff signaling her on each play what to call and whom to set. She was more accountable for carrying out the game plan. She needed to be aware of Walsh's presence, and evaluate which attacker in other zones would be most effective. If we were out of system and she had to set the ball into Walsh's zone, Fiona would set the ball slightly inside and off the net to a left side attacker who had been trained not to snap the ball down into the right side block. In the end we won the match in part because Walsh did not have a single block, even when she began switching her position on the net to try and anticipate where Fiona would set the ball.

The final stage of growth is to develop collaborative leadership, which has the potential to create a transformational relationship. This takes a lot of time and mentoring on the part of the coaching staff. Unfortunately not every player will develop to this point, but when it happens it is something special.

Collaborative leadership, whether it is with your assistant coaches or with players, means there is an open dialogue between the head coach and a player who has developed the skills and insight to help come to even better decisions. In the case of a setter, if she has the experience and intuitive intelligence to recognize what players around her are capable of in any given situation, she can sometimes make decisions which are counterintuitive (and better) than the original game plan.

This happens in the final scene in *Hoosiers*. Dale enters a huddle with a specific play in mind. The Huskers have the ball with twelve seconds on the clock. Dale plans to use Jimmy Chitwood, his best player, as a decoy. (Chitwood has rejoined the team along with the two players who walked out on the first day of practice.) Tactically it may make sense, because the opponent, South Bend Central, is likely to double team Chitwood and allow one of his teammates a much easier shot.

But the team without speaking a word, shares their opposition to Dale's decision with their body language. Instead of ignoring or becoming agitated with the team's response, Dale trusts their judgment, and after Chitwood reassures the coach he will hit the winning shot if given the opportunity, Dale calls for the team to give Chitwood the ball. This is not the decision of a broken man. It is not the decision of a head coach who is more interested in directing his team than he is in collaborating with his team. It is a decision that Dale couldn't have made at any other point in his career. He is letting go and empowering the people around him to become leaders.

Prior to shooting the final scene, Maris Valainis, playing Chitwood, had missed several shots from the top of the key, and a tired and perhaps frustrated Hackman lobbied with the director, David Ansbaugh, to let Chitwood (Valainis) take the shot from a closer distance. In an interaction which could only come from the production of this movie, Valainis persuaded Hackman and Ansbaugh he will not miss if given the opportunity to shoot from the original mark.

The film rolls for the final take. Chitwood dribbles for several seconds before planting his feet at the top of the key, lifts off the floor in slow motion and shoots, and as the ball slips over the rim and cradles in the net, hundreds of fans (movie extras who had not been told what to do) rush the floor and embrace Dale and the Hickory players with genuine affection and joy. It is hard not to respond when we sense we are in the presence of an *extraordinary* coach.

TERRY PETTIT

VICTOR, THE HAIL STORM, AND LEADERSHIP

On July 13th, a hail storm struck our neighborhood and continued for thirty minutes with an incessant pelting of .30-caliber hailstones which sent families to their basements and covered the surrounding area with an ice field that took twenty-four hours to melt. At one point the noise from the storm was so loud and so relentless that all of us: humans, dogs, and cats took to howling for relief.

When we emerged from the storm every building within sight needed a new roof. Our home also needed new gutters, window trim, and the south and west sides of our house needed repainting.

Victor Bugarin was the supervisor of a team of house painters we asked to help us. Victor and his team spent two days sanding and prepping before applying two coats of paint. The painters gave great attention to every detail. If trim needed to be repaired, they repaired it. If trim was rotten, they replaced it. If Victor could see a blemish I could not see, he repainted it. After four days, the south and west sides of our home looked like a house on the cover of a *Sunset Magazine*.

We were so impressed with the outcome we hired Victor and his team to paint the north and east sides as well, and then the kitchen ceiling and bathroom cabinets. It was not just that the house looked so much better, it was the opportunity to watch someone work at an extraordinary level. I am a fan of the extraordinary: Norah Jones; Albert Pujols; John McPhee; Northern Iowa volleyball coach, Bobbi Becker; and Victor Bugarin. I am fan of anyone who exceeds our expectations, and does it on a daily basis. That is one of the platforms of leadership.

As Victor and I were standing on our deck (the deck his team had recently restained), we began a conversation about our childhood experiences. I told Victor I grew up in Northwest Indiana, and from the age of eight my brother and I worked with my father on his milk route. It was something I couldn't appreciate at the time but it taught me skills and lessons that would become invaluable as a coach.

I told him I could not remember a time where I didn't have a part-time job as kid: selling Christmas cards and seeds in elementary school, caddying and planting gladiola bulbs in junior high, mowing fairways and greens in high school, and working in the steel mills during summer vacations from college. I told Victor that I believed having jobs as a kid was a precursor to leadership.

Victor then told me his story. He grew up twenty hours south of El Paso, Texas, in the mountains of Mexico, a place so remote that he rode a donkey one-and-a-half hours to school. After returning from school he would then load the donkey with the cheese and ice cream his mother had made by cooling the cream with river water and rotating it in cans against the cool river rocks. He would then ride the donkey another hour-and-a-half back into town where he would sell the cheese and ice cream before returning home late at night. He was six years old when he began this ritual. I decided on the spot I would be telling Victor's story in the future.

There is a book titled *Cradles of Eminence* by Victor and Mildred Goertzel which examines the childhoods of 700 of the world's most prominent people including: Martin Luther King Jr., Rosa Parks, Eleanor Roosevelt, and Helen Keller. The author identifies a handful of characteristics these leaders shared including a caring but dominating mother, and a high value on education but a dislike of schools. But the characteristic that caught my eye was they all had a job before puberty.

I first read *Cradles of Eminence* when I was mentoring coaches at the University of Nebraska where I encouraged each head coach to include the following question on the recruiting handouts to prospective student-athletes: When did you first have a job and what did you do?

If you are over fifty you might think everyone has worked somewhere before they accept an athletic scholarship, but that is not the case. At one of the universities I worked for as the director of the student-athlete leadership academy, there was not one of twenty-one team captains who had ever had a part-time job.

In a workshop for one of the teams at a different school, I asked the players to identify the most uncomfortable thing they ever had to overcome. To my shock a member of the men's golf team told me he couldn't remember ever being uncomfortable. His family owned a beer distributorship. They would fly him to Arizona so he could practice on weekends during inclement weather. Though he was recruited with a partial scholarship he rarely won a spot on the traveling team and eventually transferred back to a school near his home. When I asked the coach if he discouraged the kid from transferring he replied, "No, because he lacks a competitive spirit."

A competitive spirit may be the only thing more important than talent in the evaluation of a prospective recruit. So how do we evaluate an athlete's spirit before we make the offer? Watching as much competition as possible can give us insight into how she competes when things aren't going her way. Talking to high school and junior coaches can be helpful, although they can be inclined to market their kids rather than tell you the truth. Video can tell you whether or not a kid can't play, but unless they are one of the top recruits, they can't tell you much else.

A couple of years ago a college coach wanted my opinion on two setters she was recruiting. They each had different strengths. Both were athletic and both would probably go on to be successful college setters. I didn't watch video or ask for size or vertical jump statistics. I said, "Assuming you believe these two prospective players are relatively equal, ask yourself which one has had to overcome the most challenges to put herself in the position to be recruited? That is the one I would want running my offense."

And if she had ridden a donkey to school, or paid for her own club expenses, or sold eggs at a farm stand, or ice cream at the Dairy Maid, I would offer her a scholarship in a heartbeat, because there is a very good chance I would be getting a two for one deal: setting and leadership. Victor agrees.

TERRY PETTIT

THOUGHTS, QUESTIONS, AND RECOMMENDATIONS

• I have spent the last seven months floating in the debris field called club volleyball. I jumped in with both feet as the head coach of a sixteen-and-under team, armed with two talented assistants, and ten hardworking players from local high schools. To my surprise I enjoyed coaching club volleyball as much as I enjoyed coaching at the collegiate level, partly because I had the opportunity to coach our youngest daughter, but also because coaching is, well . . . coaching.

• Every international and collegiate women's coach I have talked with believes it is a tremendous advantage for volleyball players to continue to play other sports in their developmental years, yet we have club programs that either do not allow or discourage athletes to continue to develop other neural pathways through competition in sports other than volleyball. Are these programs ignoring experience and science or is control more important to them than the long-term success of the athlete?

• The border between Pakistan and Afghanistan is a great metaphor for junior volleyball. Clubs are tribes, each of them have different goals, motives and power bases. Perhaps the U.S.A. Volleyball, Amateur Athletic Union, or Junior Volleyball Directors Association could provide information to help parents become better consumers. Some of us spend more time and less money researching a used Honda we buy for our kid than we do the junior program we are sending them to.

• I am most impressed with junior coaches who have a background in high school coaching and educational psychology. They understand the needs and responsibilities of their players beyond volleyball and the different ways people learn. I am least impressed with coaches, who though passionate about volleyball, have not invested the time or energy to gain insight into coaching women in team sport. Their vision of coaching sometimes does not go beyond scrimmaging, frequently with the coach playing on the other side of the net.

• Every club or organization that bids to host a qualifier should be required to submit a plan for distributing 15 percent of the profit to the development of low income and minority players within the region where the qualifier is located, and another 5 percent of the profit should go to the USAV for specific projects which have the same goal. The availability of our game to minority athletes is as embarrassingly low as the profits to be made from hosting a qualifier are high.

• The NCAA should consider legislation allowing an institution to award a thirteenth scholarship in women's volleyball or an extra scholarship in men's volleyball if that institution has awarded a specific number of scholarships to minority athletes during the previous three seasons (five in women's volleyball, and three partials in men's volleyball). Schools that do not have the resources to pay for a thirteenth scholarship should have the opportunity to apply for a special grant to be funded by the NCAA. Don't get caught up in the formula here. What matters is if there are specific scholarship dollars available for minority athletes, then club volleyball will adjust accordingly and begin to recruit and train those athletes for collegiate play.

• The greatest predictor for volleyball success in high school and college is size. The second is arm-speed. If a club can only take a limited number of players in its entry-level stages, club directors and coaches should do everything possible to keep taller girls involved even when they may not be as skilled or as coordinated as smaller kids at an early age.

• Finally, I believe in addition to volleyball fundamentals, junior coaches have a responsibility to teach the kids we work with how to be *coachable*, not to just their junior coach or club, but to future coaches they will have the opportunity to work with in their high school, junior, and collegiate careers. Our goal is not to become the final authority on how the game is played, but to encourage them to take risks, be open-minded and to be great team members after their association with us has ended.

TERRY PETTIT

NOTES FROM LOUISVILLE:

Home to Muhammad Ali, Turned Hard Maple, and the Host City for the 2012 NCAA Division I Women's Volleyball Championship

At the Louisville Slugger Museum and Bat Factory, located five blocks west of the YUM! Center, the venue for the 2012 NCAA Division I Women's Volleyball Championship, there is an exhibit designed to let visitors see what a ninety mile per hour fastball looks like. After pushing a button, a video of Cole Hamels, a left-handed pitcher for the Philadelphia Phillies, winds up and appears to throw a live fastball which is actually released from a pitching machine hidden beneath his image.

I watched as pitch after pitch struck a padded target behind the plate, each pitch thrown for a strike with the same velocity, before I decided to walk around behind the batters' box to see what a major league fastball looked like from the batter's perspective behind a glass wall.

On the very first pitch, the ball left Hamels' left hand and struck the glass in front of my face. My immediate thought, after checking to see if my left cheek had shattered, was that I would never move fast enough to get out of the way. My second thought was that the pitch Hamels threw at me was an *outlier*.

I looked at the glass where the ball struck and noticed there were a dozen marks that indicated the wayward pitch had happened several times before. My suspicion is that the problem is not with the pitching machine but that one of the balls had a cut or imperfection which caused the ball to move in a different pattern when it is loaded into the machine in just the right way.

An outlier is a behavior which lies outside the normal pattern of distribution. The term became popular with the publication of Malcolm Gladwell's bestseller *Outliers,* which shares several theories about why certain events happen, from the unusually high percentage of January birthdates for professional hockey players to a convincing argument on why a well-respected airline suffered a higher percentage of catastrophic events.

The 2012 Oregon volleyball team that advanced through the Nebraska Regional and defeated Penn State in the second national semifinal in Louisville had all the requirements for outlier status. The Ducks were last in the Pac-12 in blocking; a skill which is usually a requirement to go deep into the tournament, and their athletic talent was uneven when compared with teams like Texas, Penn State, and other programs who frequent the championship finals.

The Ducks did have an exceptional setter in five foot nine junior All-American Lauren Plum whose ability to set her primary target, six foot three senior outside hitter Alaina Bergsma on what appeared to be a rope from anywhere on the court. That tempo allowed Bergsma to average close to five kills per game, while earning Pac-12 Player of the Year honors and enabled the Ducks to hit at a stellar .289 attack percentage while playing in one of the toughest conferences in the country.

The tempo of the sets that came out of Plum's hands were so fast that even when the Ducks were out of system the Penn State block was slow to organize against Oregon's outside hitters. How much difference does that make? I would go so far as to say that had Oregon run a traditional offense similar to many of the teams they defeated in the tournament, the Ducks might not have been in the tournament in the first place. Oregon head coach Jim Moore concurred.

Moore believes playing with a traditional tempo, when the teams you have to beat have taller or more athletic players, is like giving up. He also believes there is less risk of an unforced error in setting a quick-tempo set to a *trained* outside hitter than the traditional higher set that most college teams use when they are in system. When I asked Stanford head coach John Dunning what he thought was the key to Oregon's success, he answered, "Jim believes so strongly in what he is doing offensively, that eventually his players come to believe in it as well."

Consider this: Bergsma and Oregon's two other outside hitters, six foot one sophomore Liz Brenner and five foot ten senior Katherine Fisher, combined for forty-nine kills in four sets against Penn State. (I would guess no pin hitters have had that kind of success against Penn State in the last six years.) It was not that the Nittany Lions didn't know where the ball was going; it was that until you have seen the tempo that Oregon runs its offense, it is hard for players to understand how quickly they must close the block even when the setter is twenty-five feet off the net.

Texas defeated Michigan, a program that has quietly eliminated Stanford from the NCAA Tournament in three of the last four years, in a very competitive five-set match in the first semifinal. Texas then had the advantage of watching the tempo of the Oregon offense before the two teams met in the final match.

Texas also had the advantage of having several well-trained, extraordinary athletes who were playing at a higher level than anyone else in the month of December, and who sustained that excellence into the championship match. There the Longhorns, under the leadership of head coach Jerritt Elliott, won their first NCAA National Division I Volleyball Championship since 1988 by defeating Oregon, 25-11, 26-24, and 25-19.

Six foot one senior right side attacker Sha'dare McNeal, six foot one sophomore middle blocker Khat Bell, six foot three sophomore outside hitter Haley Eckerman, and the tournament MVP, six foot three junior outside hitter Bailey Webster, were recruited by many of the top programs, but Texas has created a culture which has enabled the Longhorns to recruit and develop extraordinary minority athletes that is the envy of collegiate coaches. Those four athletes combined for thirty-eight of Texas' forty-three kills in the championship match while committing only four attack errors.

Undoubtedly some of that recruiting success is due to the talents of associate head coach and recruiting coordinator Salima Rockwell, a former All-American setter and assistant coach at Penn State. But Elliott deserves credit for hiring Rockwell, and just as importantly, for keeping Rockwell when every other school in the country with a head coach opening would like to woo her to take charge of their program.

Texas, like Penn State, has been able to recruit several minority athletes to its roster who have played significant roles in their championship seasons, at a time when a limited number of minority athletes are choosing to play college volleyball. The costs associated with club volleyball and the lack of a comprehensive plan to make our sport available to minorities and athletes from low-income families continues to be one of the factors which makes a team with the diversity of Texas an outlier as well.

SHOULD VOLLEYBALL COACHES PACK MORE THAN CLIPBOARDS?

The big question on everyone's mind is, "Should we arm head coaches?" I have thought about this a great deal and have come to the following talking points.

I don't think it is a good idea to strap a sidearm onto a head coach during competition or the two days before or after a competition. There are too many times in my own coaching career when I became unstable, many of them situations which you would recognize:

- Someone serves into the bottom of the net at match point.
- A video of an opponent arrives when it is too late to view it before the competition.
- The players not in the match are playing grab-ass at the end of the bench.
- The assistant coaches are playing grab-ass at the end of the bench.
- At a critical point in the set my serving specialist serves number seven, the player I just identified as the person not to serve.

It is important to realize during this discussion that "guns don't kill people, people do." I am not a logician so when I run across a statement like this I like to substitute another situation to see if the logic holds up.

"Heroine doesn't kill people, people do."

"Driving 175 miles per hour down the interstate doesn't kill people, people do."

"Second hand cigarette smoke doesn't kill people, people do."

"Unforced errors don't end a coaching career, people do."

Because I have an unstable personality I will leave it to you to come up with your own conclusions.

In any case I probably would arm the second assistant before I strapped a holster onto the head coach, at least if the head coach is a male. A gun only looks cool if you are dressed for the part. Female head coaches qualify. Almost all female head coaches look like they spent considerable time choosing what to wear before a match. Some of them even wear heels, which I am particularly fond of. It would be especially cool if a female head coach wore a holster with a pearl- handled Colt 45 facing the wrong way, requiring her to reach across her body before drawing the revolver.

Male coaches should not wear a holster for several reasons. First of all, most male head volleyball coaches dress as if they are selling Craftsmen tools at Sears. A few wear sweat pants, because to them, coaching is training, and they are always training. Unfortunately this comes across on TV as if the head coach just attended an adult sleepover.

Male coaches are also much more likely to be mentally ill, a state of mind which has been targeted by the National Rifle Association as the primary reason the United States wins the gold in gun deaths among "civilized nations."

Female head coaches, unlike their male counterparts, do not refuse to shake hands after competition, do not wear hoodies, do not chew tobacco (a stimulant), do not bump into the opposing head coach when turning in their lineup, and they do it all, hopefully, in high heels while doing that Ginger Rogers thing.

But someone has to be armed, because Wayne LaPierre, Executive Vice President and Chief Executive Officer of the National Rifle Association, keeps reminding us, "The only way to stop a bad guy with a gun is to have a good guy with a gun." (I tried to substitute the word "dynamite"for "gun" to test the logic of this thinking but it left me confused.)

If we aren't going to arm the head coach, that leaves assistant coaches, referees, the scorekeeper, the libero tracker, lines people, concessionaires, fans, and indigent people who have come in out of the rain as possibilities.

Personally I would rule out fans. Fan is an abbreviation for the word fanatic. I would also rule out parents (too much opportunity for injury by friendly fire). With twenty-seven subs, when you count the libero entries, I wouldn't give the scorekeeper or libero tracker added responsibility. Concessionaires have line-of-site issues. There has to be another option.

What about Federal Air Marshals? First of all they can't be flying all the time. I think of myself as a fairly perceptive person, being that I once identified more than twenty shore birds in a round of golf, and I've never identified a Federal Air Marshal on a flight I was a passenger on. So they're available. But come to think of it I've never seen any gun violence on a flight I've been on, and I've been on some flights with a passenger or two whom I thought had crossed the line from neurotic to crazy. I'm hesitant to draw any conclusions, but it appears most passengers seem to be regulated into being good guys.

Maybe we should play all of our matches inside abandoned 787 jets (which may soon be available), or better yet design our arenas so they have the same feel, ambience, and regulations a flight from Omaha to Denver enjoys. We could have uncomfortable seats that recline into our neighbor's laps, single-stall bathrooms with smoke monitors, enjoy tiny packets of peanuts and pretzels and teeny cups of apple juice. We could pretend, just like in real life, there is an air marshal somewhere in the building. The good guys wouldn't have to pack anything more than a box of popcorn and the male head coaches could be as professional as their female counterparts and dress as well as a co-pilot on a regional airline. That would be progress.

TERRY PETTIT

DEAR MR. VOLLEYBALL KNOW-IT-ALL

Dear Mr. Volleyball Know-It-All: I am the coach at Alaska-Gates of the Arctic University. We would like to host the NCAA Women's Division I Volleyball Championship in 2018. We have an 18,000 seat outdoor arena. The wind chill in mid-December can approach minus sixty-five degrees and there is always the possibility of a civilian being hit by a twenty-ton ice road trucker on the way to the match. There is not a strong volleyball community here but I would like to introduce championship volleyball to the region. Do you think we have a chance of hosting?

Mr. Volleyball Know-It-All: *That depends upon the makeup of the Division I volleyball committee. Sometimes they choose established volleyball communities and sometimes they take a more "missionary" attitude and select places like Richmond, Virginia, and Cleveland, Ohio. If their goal is the latyer, you've got a chance.*

Dear Mr. Volleyball Know-It-All: My athletic director wants me to carry twenty-eight players on my roster so our crappy football team can continue to have 118 players on its roster. What do you think of this?

Mr. Volleyball Know-It-All: *I think you should be very happy. Per Title IX, if football teams had a roster of forty players, women's volleyball, women's golf, women's tennis, women's field hockey, and women's soccer teams would become club sports.*

Dear Mr. Volleyball Know-It-All: I read the volleyball rules committee is considering replacing the fifteen-point fifth set, with a game of "Red Rover." What's up with that?

Mr. Volleyball Know-It-All: *NCAA committees like to change things to justify their existence and the hardship of meeting in Key West and Palm Springs. Substitutions have gone from twelve to eighteen back to twelve then to fifteen in recent years.*

Dear Mr. Volleyball Know-It-All: Why is it that volleyball referees and umpires have gotten so crabby?

Mr. Volleyball Know-It-All: *I think officials feel underappreciated, and sometimes they grow tired of having a coach who has his pants on backwards screaming about a double hit. A few of them also believe that club and collegiate volleyball should have the decorum of an Olympic qualifier.*

Dear Mr. Volleyball Know-It-All: The university I coach at has changed conferences five times in the last ten years. Sometimes we don't even play a season in the new conference before we move to the next conference. What's behind this craziness?

Mr. Volleyball Know-It-All: *Three reasons: Fox Sports, ESPN, and Silas Marner.*

Dear Mr. Volleyball Know-It-All: The University of Kentucky has built a dormitory for its men's basketball team with amenities that rival a Hyatt. This would seem to be a clear violation of NCAA rules. What's up?

Mr. Volleyball Know-It-All: *The NCAA is fighting for its life. It is afraid at any moment the BCS schools will form their own organization, complete with bowl playoffs, cheating scandals, and a basketball championship tournament with revenues that rival the University of Texas' athletic budget. The NCAA is backing-off on enforcement, recruiting calendars, and limitations on phone contacts because it doesn't want to offend any of the major players. The new NCAA motto is: "We are all Miami."*

Dear Mr. Volleyball Know-It-All: What do you think of recruiting transfer students from other schools?

Mr. Volleyball Know-It-All: *Thirty years ago a "transfer" could be a poor student, a malcontent, or someone who robbed a convenient store. Now it is more likely to be someone who doesn't get enough playing time or someone the head coach doesn't want to take the time to develop. Secondary recruiting has become as important in college sports as the recruiting of high school seniors. I'm not sure a volleyball program without a tradition can move into the top fifty teams without recruiting foreign athletes or being open to selective transfers.*

Dear Mr. Volleyball Know-It-All: What is the most important factor beyond talent in building a successful program?

Mr. Volleyball Know-It-All: *Relating to players. I've never met a head coach who didn't think he or she related well with their players, but in reality many of us don't. We have ways to measure passing, attack efficiency, and side-out percentages but most of us do not have the tools to measure (beyond wins and losses or changed behavior) whether or not we relate well with our staff and student-athletes. There may be coaches who are naturally good at relating, but I suspect the best relaters are head coaches who have made it a priority to learn from educational psychology, mentors, peers, and assistant coaches who have been granted freedom and safety to share their opinions on what they see happening in the communication between a head coach and a team. Being available is a good start.*

Dear Mr. Volleyball Know-It-All: We have spent thousands of dollars on club volleyball. This year we paid for three sets of uniforms, matching sweatshirts for parents, hair ties, travel to two qualifiers and six regional events, a high performance tryout, a Canon Rebel camera and an iPad with digital editing, lodging at "stay and play hotels," admission to qualifiers, parking for qualifiers, salty snacks, fried doughnuts and jungle juice, pocket tacos, a folding table and crock pot, ankle braces, knee pads, Neosporin, a recruiting service, and now we have to go to junior nationals because we finished in seventh in a qualifier but the four teams above us had already qualified. We can't afford it, but our club director says if we don't go none of the girls in North Dakota can ever play volleyball again. What do you think?

Mr. Volleyball Know-It-All: *I understand your dilemma. U.S.A. Volleyball funds its national teams from club volleyball registrations, qualifiers, high-performance tryouts, donations, and junior nationals. It is a little bit like the Cleveland Indians funding their baseball team from Little League receipts. I think most kids and families would be better served by taking a break from volleyball after playing from December through May, while hopefully still competing in other high school sports and activities. It is not likely to happen. U.S.A. Volleyball needs the revenue from a national tournament. Some club directors need to keep kids in their facilities to justify healthy fees and pay for utilities, and many of us continue to propogate the old lies; that it is better for young kids to specialize in one sport, and that rest is not a part of a healthy training regimen.*

THE TOP TEN THINGS
I WISH I HAD KNOWN AS
A FRESHMAN COLLEGIATE ATHLETE

A column written by Emma Pettit

1.   The recruiting period is over. This means your new coach, who seemed so likable and held you in such high regard, is no longer obligated to tell you how good you are. You traded in your last bargaining chip when you decided to come to this school. Now it's the coach's turn to mold you into a player he can use. This means that most conversations are not focused on what you're doing well, but on what you need to do better. This also means there is direct critical feedback, sometimes in the form of shouting. Remember that all of your teammates go through this. If this gets to be too much then review point #9: *Don't be afraid to cry.*

2.   The coaches will probably be somewhat different than you imagined them to be. This is not necessarily a bad thing. That super nice, smiley guy you met on the recruiting trips probably wouldn't be able to create the top-notch team you wanted to be a part of anyway. Try to reserve your judgment until the end of the season, and then try to reserve it to the end of the off-season . . . and then keep withholding judgment until the end of your college career. Because if you're like me, you have a coach who is right a lot more than you want them to be and you don't want to admit that to yourself quite yet. So respect the decisions your coaches make; even if you've heard it a thousand times, they probably know best.

3.   Being a good teammate doesn't just mean being a good player. So many college freshmen think their job is done once practice is over, but really being a good teammate means so much more than that. It means encouraging others even if they are competing for the same position as you. It means showing up early to help set up the nets, even if it's not your job. It means studying and getting good grades so your coaches aren't anxious about your eligibility. Even if you're not playing, or even close to playing, you can always be a good teammate.

4.   You will always be overwhelmingly exhausted, even on your occasional day off when you haven't moved out of your bed since you woke up three hours ago.

5.   But also remember you will never be as exhausted as your team captain. Your team captain doesn't walk when she shags balls; she runs. She knows to finish first in every punishment run, and she knows her collegiate career is coming to a close so she holds on to every drill as tightly as possible. You, on the other hand, do not know this. You are actually pretty clueless about the whole thing. On top of everything else the team captain has to worry about, she also has to make sure you and the other freshmen don't screw up too badly. So please, cut her some slack.

6.   There is no social life during season. You might want to go to a party, meet new people, or even stay up past 11:00 p.m., but all of this changes when you're playing Notre Dame the next day and you need your full eight hours. It's okay; the parties your classmates rave about are probably not that great (or at least that's what you tell yourself because it's not like you'll ever get to go anyway).

7.   Since you don't really have a social life, this makes your teammates even more important. They are now the people you spend over 70 percent of your time with. They will be your best friends, the bridesmaids or groomsmen at your wedding. You may not be super close with all of them, but it is your job to develop at least a respectful relationship

with each person, even if you "don't get where they're coming from" sometimes. It doesn't matter. Just like you can't choose family, you can't choose teammates. But you love them anyway.

8.   You will look like crap a lot. Sweatpants are your new best friend and everyone else is just going to have to accept that.

9.   You will cry at some point. I don't care if you're starting, have a ton of new friends, and good grades. At some point things will overwhelm you and you will cry. It's okay, if it's happening to you, you can bet it's happening to some of your freshmen teammates. Talk to them about it. You don't have to fake like you have it together all the time . . . unless your coach is walking by. Then you should probably wipe those tears and stop sniffling.

10. The season is ridiculously long. You'll actually feel yourself graying and wrinkling, the season seems so long. There will be days where you would rather have a root canal operated on than go to practice. Soreness is your new normal, and you've even entertained thoughts of quitting, but then finally the last day comes and of course you're sad, but you're mainly relieved. You think to yourself, I don't know if I could have gone one week longer. Then you go back to your dorm, go to bed, wake up the next morning, and want to play again. You'll go to the gym or field just to hit the ball around and break up these now incredibly boring days that don't have practice in the middle of them. You'll linger around your coaches' offices because you actually miss them. This is how you know you made the right decision.

If after all those practices and the traveling and the meetings and the crying . . . if after all that you still find yourself missing freshman season the minute after it ended, you know you were meant to play in college. You're at the right place. You'll be okay.

Emma Pettit
Villanova Volleyball
Class of 2016

TWELVE THINGS I WOULD DO
IF I WERE STILL COACHING
COLLEGE VOLLEYBALL

1. Even though fifteen subs plus a libero allows coaches to specialize in the back row, I would continue to train all-around players for two reasons: first, having a core group of players who are always on the court encourages accountability and leadership. I also want to have a strong back row attack option in every rotation. Secondly, I would prefer to have at least four of my players on the court in every rotation because I believe more all-around players creates more stability. That means with the setter and the libero, two other position players need to play in both the front and back row.

2. I would be searching for more ways players could take care of themselves with regard to preparing for practice. Baseball does the best job of this with the players being responsible for the care of the field. Players would set up and take down the nets, carry water, etc. The manager would be just that: she would "manage" the players' responsibilities. I don't believe creating a "celebrity" culture results in leadership.

3. I do not think serving is consistently tough at the collegiate level, especially when compared to the top servers internationally. If you want to play in the back row for my team you to need to have at least one forcing serve and you need to be able to serve short under pressure. I also have to give you the time and coaching to develop those skills.

4. I do not see enough "teaching" going on during competition. I would place one of my assistant coaches at the end of the bench with the players, teaching them how to watch the game, discern patterns, and make adjustments. Not teaching during competition is wasting an opportunity for players to develop the mental side of the game.

5. Talent is a given. We cannot compete without talent. Having said that, I would spend more time trying to identify whether or not potential recruits have the qualities necessary to contribute to the culture we are building. Some of the qualities I am looking for are:

- Integrity
- Curiosity
- A willingness to be uncomfortable
- Passion
- Competitiveness

6. There are three questions I want answered before I know whether or not I can successfully coach a person:

- What are you motivated by?
- How do you learn?
- Are you coachable?

7. One of greatest predictors of potential leadership is a job before puberty. I want to know the following:

- What was your first job?
- What have you done to take care of yourself?
- When have you chosen to be uncomfortable to reach a goal?

8. If I were fortunate enough to be coaching in a program that consistently qualified for the conference or NCAA National Championship tournaments, I would try to alter my perspective accordingly. I would be less concerned with having every question answered early in the season even if that meant a higher possibility of

losing an early-season match. I would prefer to not have surprises in November. I understand programs trying to break through to get into the tournament for the first time may not be able to be this patient.

9. The player who is more likely to work through challenges when things are not going her way is a person who has chosen a school for more than just volleyball. Volleyball may be the most important reason, but it also helps if she has grown up with a dream that goes beyond whether or not she starts, redshirts, or plays a different role than she anticipated. I don't need twelve stars to build a great team. I may need three or four stars, but I also need an equal number of players who would give their left arm to be a part of that team no matter what happens.

10. One of my leaders would be my libero. I want her to believe (like my setter) she is at the center of why we are successful. She has to be an extraordinary passer, capable of playing any back row position, with the skills and understanding of the game that I would expect from a great setter. The libero is my side-out captain. The setter is my transition captain. Whether or not my libero and my setter lead verbally is not as important as leading with their consistent play and mindset.

11. I would train and play multiple defensive base positions depending upon the strengths of the opponent and whether or not the opponent is siding-out or in transition. If the situation warranted it I would have my libero switch to a different back row position if I thought the percentages warranted making the switch at a critical point in the match.

12. I would try to find a way for my team to have a four to five day break from practice, twice during the season. I believe people learn more efficiently when they have periodic breaks to assimilate the information and movement patterns they are being trained in. An ideal cycle would be a break every five and one-half weeks. I know that is probably not possible, but I would try to find a way to come as close to it as I could.

TERRY PETTIT

A LETTER TO TEAM MEMBERS
ON THE BRINK OF A NEW SEASON

As we begin the fall season I wanted to address the behaviors that will give us the opportunity to have the most success this season.

We have twelve very competitive people on our team. I anticipate a regular rotation of nine players: a setter, a libero, two middle blockers, two left side hitters, a right side player, and two defensive specialists. That leaves three players that will provide depth or who might also be situational substitutions. Some of you will be in roles you have dreamed of and some of you may be challenged with a position or role that is unfamiliar.

Your competitive spirit is one of the primary reasons you were recruited to this team. One of your responsibilities is to compete as hard as you can for a position on the court. Another responsibility is to cheer and support your teammates as hard as you can when you are not on the court. These behaviors are not options to consider, but rather the DNA of our culture.

If we are to have a successful season, we will not be the same team in December as we are now. Having said that, teams do not develop or get better by just announcing their intent to do so. Teams get better when individuals commit to behaviors that leverage their strengths and address their weaknesses. This is much harder than it sounds because it requires a level of consistent commitment much greater than anything you have ever done. It also requires courage and the willingness to be uncomfortable for long periods of time.

Some of you will be asked to change footwork patterns. Some of you will be asked to communicate in a more assertive voice. Some of you will be asked to alter your posture or become more dynamic in your approach. All of you will be asked to perform and execute when you are fatigued. Your improvement may not be in a straight line, but if we are to be successful, your commitment to new behaviors has to be unwavering. If you do not make that commitment now you are likely to let go when fatigue, injury, or doubt enter the equation.

Talent is a given. You would not be here if the coaching staff did not believe you have the talent to compete and excel at this level. Talent combined with being coachable is our base position. In fact, being coachable may even be more important than being talented.

The coaching staff is charged with training you in your movement patterns, your fundamentals, your understanding of the game, and your adjustments, to such a degree, that you can respond as quickly as possible during competition without thinking. This requires perfect or *deliberate* practice, which requires repetition and error correction. This is not always fun. Fun is defeating a worthy opponent because you are prepared.

A great example of our preparation is our commitment to our base position. Base position is not just a place on the court where we are positioned to defend overpasses, setter attacks, and quick attacks. It is also a commitment to posture, attitude, recognizing situations, and being persistent.

Great players (also known as great teams) *love* working to be in base position and they are as alert to the possibilities that might occur in the middle of the third set as they are at the beginning of the match. Average teams skate to a position on the court but as the match evolves their posture and their alertness begin to wane. Great teams can change their base position and make adjustments on the fly or as directed by the coaching staff. Average teams are locked into a specific place on the court.

We are a talented team, but we may play several teams that have more athletic talent than we do. We will, however, not play any team who has a stronger commitment to the behaviors that lead to championship volleyball than we do. These behaviors include, but are not exclusive to our commitment to:

- Our decision to be coachable
- Our competitiveness
- Our eye contact when communicating with teammates and coaches
- Our communication on every contact
- Our understanding of *how* we can be successful
- Our alertness on the court and while waiting to be on the court
- Our trust that if we are relentless in our training, we will get better
- Our understanding that while great volleyball is deceptively simple, it is one of the hardest and most rewarding things to accomplish

If we can do all of these things with a consistent passion for getting better, and do it not just for ourselves but because we are lucky enough to have teammates who have also made this commitment, we will have made the first step in moving from talented to extraordinary. Embrace the opportunity with your teammates and coaches!

TERRY PETTIT

YIKES: A CHECKLIST FOR HIGH SCHOOL RECRUITS AND THEIR PARENTS

There are several decisions and evaluations a recruited high school athlete and her parents have to make during the recruiting process. Among those are the following:

• *What level of college volleyball can I play and have success at?*

Both you and your parents may need some help with this one. While your high school or club coach may be of help, sometimes they don't have much experience with the recruiting process, and unfortunately there are some coaches who may want you to go to the most prestigious school or division because it makes their own program look good. The key is not necessarily to be recruited to the highest division or the strongest volleyball school but to get a *great fit*.

A great fit is a school and level of play in which you can thrive at, be challenged in a healthy environment, and experience some success. Sometimes it helps to get an opinion from a college coach who is not recruiting you, but has seen you compete several times, or from another high school or club coach who has had experience with recruiting in college volleyball.

• *How important is the prospect of significant playing time in my decision?*

It would be hard to overestimate the importance of playing time. It is extremely difficult to put in hundreds of hours for four-to-five years without having a realistic chance of being on the court. As one of my coaching friends says, "It is like being a salmon swimming upstream." There are a few who can do it, but most of us need the reward of playing. Be honest with yourself on this question. If you could embrace the prospect of sitting on the bench of a very successful program and provide support in practice so that team can reach its goals, then this option becomes a possibility. But if you need to play to make this journey possible, then move that reality up toward the top of the list in your requirements for a rewarding college experience.

• *Can I reach my academic goals at the institution I am considering, and does the athletic department have the support services to help me reach those goals?*

Volleyball is a means to an end. Five years from now the most important thing will be that you received a great education and a degree, which will put you in position to lead a productive life as an adult. This is more likely to happen if the school you choose has an academic program you are passionate about and has the academic support to give you the best chance for success.

• *Under what "type" of coaching do I learn and perform my best?*

Collegiate coaching is much stronger today for women's sports than it was thirty years ago because the typical college coach today is much more experienced than his or her predecessors. Some coaches get results by directing players, others by collaborating with them. Some coaches make an effort to recognize how different players learn while some coaches expect the players to do the adjusting. It is not necessary for you to be "comfortable" with everything a head coach does because part of her job is to make you "uncomfortable" as she coaches you toward your potential.

Make a point of watching at least one or two practices before you make up your mind. Watch how the head coach interacts with both the best players on the team and the players who receive the least amount of playing time. You are likely to be in both of those roles during your collegiate career, and it is easier to move from one role to the other if the head coach values the efforts of everyone.

- *Do the assistant coaches at the schools I am considering compliment the strengths and limitations of the head coach?*

Nobody has it all. There are coaches who are great technicians and coaches who are better recruiters than trainers. There are coaches who are great communicators and coaches who stop communicating once you commit. There are coaches who are dictatorial and coaches who want to play a guitar before matches. There are coaches who are consistent and coaches who have a completely different personality on game day. All of these coaches with all of these limitations can develop teams who have success if they have surrounded themselves with assistant coaches who have different talents.

Steer clear of programs which appear to have clones for a coaching staff. There needs to be at least one person on the staff who is great at relating to players. There needs to be at least one person on the staff who is great at developing talent. There needs to be at least one person on the staff who knows there are other things in life beyond volleyball. There needs to be at least one person on the staff who has been empowered by the head coach to say, "You know, maybe we should consider another way to do this."

- *How important is it for me to be in a program that "develops" talent as opposed to a program that recruits players with more experience than I have and focuses more on team play than technical training?*

Every head coach has the goal of trying to recruit talent better than the players he already has. Therefore, it is in your best interest to choose a program that develops talent so you will be playing your best volleyball as an upperclassman. When you evaluate a college program, ask yourself: do the players at this school seem to peak early in their college careers or are they continuing to get better in their senior year?

Burnout happens when a player senses she is no longer improving. Great coaches find ways to motivate and challenge players to continue to improve their games throughout their college career.

• *What is the history of players transferring in and out of the programs I am considering?*

There are more players transferring today than ever before in collegiate athletics. By one estimate, close to 40 percent of male collegiate basketball players are at a second school before the end of their sophomore year. We have not approached those percentages in college volleyball but the majority of NCAA Division I schools are likely to have one or two players transfer in or out every couple of years. What you want to avoid is choosing a program that has a pattern of running kids off because they don't perform or because the coach wants to have a scholarship available for a better player.

Of course this is a two-way street. If you want a coach to remain committed to you, then you (or your parents) shouldn't see a scholarship as a way to prove yourself so you can transfer at the first opportunity to a stronger program. It is in your best interest to wait until you have thoroughly researched the program you are committing to and why it may not be wise to verbally commit before you can legally drive a car or go to *Hangover IV*.

You and your interests are going to change significantly from your freshman year in high school through the beginning of your senior year. It will take tremendous maturity for both you and your parents not to jump when you get the offer of a scholarship early in your high school career. But if a head coach likes you that much, he will certainly like you just as much two years later, and you will have a much better idea of who you are becoming and who can help you develop in all facets of your life.

• *Do I have complete trust the head coach is concerned about the well-being of her players beyond what they can do for her on the volleyball court?*

Trust is everything in a player-coach relationship and first impressions are not always accurate. I would tend to not trust anyone who tries to control my decision by telling me I have to commit during my unofficial visit, or by a specific date during my sophomore year, or who threatens to offer the scholarship to another person if I don't commit tonight. Look at it this way: you would never buy a Scion or Honda Civic under those circumstances and the decision about where you spend your college years is a lot more important than purchasing a car.

If a head coach tries to bully you into an early commitment then he will likely bully you in other ways when you are part of the team. Explore all the opportunities you are really interested in, but don't waste your time and a school's money by visiting a program you have no intent on attending.

You probably aren't going to have a head coach tell you what you don't want to hear. You are more likely to get a good feel for who a head coach is by watching her or him in practice, by watching how he handles great play and less-than-good play, and how he interacts in competition with players who are both successful and those who struggle.

- *What if NCAA Division I schools or my favorite schools don't recruit me?*

What if Justin Bieber doesn't ask you out on a date? Volleyball can be just as much fun at the NCAA Division II, III, NAIA, or junior college level, and another division may actually meet more of your needs. There are more than a 1,500 schools playing college volleyball at various levels and your job is to find a place where you can contribute. Your college experience is going to be determined more by the relationships you develop with your teammates and the culture of the program you choose than by whether or not you play in front of 3,000 people or your parent's alma mater. Make a decision to have a great college experience at a school where you can play a significant role.

TERRY PETTIT

A REPORT FROM LINCOLN

It is late spring in Lincoln, Nebraska.
The dogwoods planted in backyard gardens,
The pear trees on the boulevard,
The plum bushes in wild thickets at the edge of town,
Have already blossomed.

Sunlight comes early and goes home late.
We are ten days from the summer equinox
When the "Big Boys" and "Better Boys" we planted in clay pots
Will get sixteen hours of sunlight.

The first heat wave of the summer has arrived . . .
The mayor has asked us to water our lawns on alternate days.
A voice on the radio tells us that out in the country
Prairie grasses are more combustible than gasoline.

A few weeks ago there was graduation.
We had a reception and attended others
With bright punch and small rectangular pieces of cake.
At one of the baccalaureates there was an empty seat for a classmate
Who did not survive a horrible automobile crash,
And whom we will continue to think about years after
We have sent our own children to college.

TERRY PETTIT

This is an interesting time if you are eighteen years old
Living on the rim of adulthood in Lincoln, Nebraska.
Life can best be explained by imagining two funnels
Lying opposite each other with their stems connected.
In the first funnel are all the challenges you have survived,
The pain of peer pressure, acne, and bad locker partners.
The meanness that comes from friends in junior high.
The time you took the last shot . . . and missed.
The times you wondered if there were too many expectations.

Some nights were spent wondering whether we will ever be loved
By anyone other than our parents,
Who, as everyone knows, are required by state law to love us,
Who are also required to remind us of this fact
Each time they don't give us something we want,
And who continually ask us where we are going
Even when we aren't.

And just where are we going anyway?
To the U, St. Cloud State, Wesleyan, and Duke.
Some place where no adult is going to ask us about what we are wearing
Or whether or not we have something on our mind.
Some place where we don't have to share anything
With a goofy brother or sister
Whom we may secretly start to miss.

The next few years, where the two stems meet, is a sanctuary
Where you get to try different things on.
You can try on architecture or criminal justice.
You can try on journalism or marine biology
Even if you've only been to the ocean on the Internet.

You can try on new friends.
You can read short stories by William Faulkner till morning
And sing loud songs on the toilet.
You can try out new ideas.

You can be a Buddhist for a semester.
You can give up meat or lettuce.
You can take a course in African pottery.
You can break the rules.
You can choose to not make your bed.
You can wear colors that don't match
And flip-flops to class.
You can sleep in on Wednesday mornings,
And you can choose not to go out for drama,
Speech and debate, student council, French club, and track.

You can also choose to do all of those things if you really want.
You can adopt a highway with friends
Or a cat by yourself . . . as long as the head resident doesn't see it.
You can cut your fingernails and let them fly through the air
As they somersault to the carpet . . . and not pick them up.

In the other funnel at the end of the stems, hard things await.
It will be hard to stay passionate about a job.
It will be hard, at times, to stay healthy.
It will be hard to lose weight.
It will be hard to find the right companion.
It will be hard to stay married.
It will be hard to say no to your daughter
When you have the means to give her what she wants.
It will be hard to be a teacher, a clerk, a coach, or an actuary.
The hardest thing of all will be to be a good parent.
It's hard not to step in and try to make things easy
When your daughter needs to find out some answers for herself.
It is hard to let your children experience the pain of growing up.

But there will be things not so hard as well . . .
Like what is happening to your parents at this moment:

Mom and Dad are taking a deep breath.
They are telling themselves how all your problems were small.

Nothing that couldn't be fixed with discussion or duct tape.
They are thinking back to when you were five or six
Playing t-ball and micro soccer
And how, out of all those kids that you did everything with,
You were the one who continued . . .
Who continued to compete,
Who continued to get good grades,
Who continued to make good decisions,
Who continued to move toward something outside yourself.
Now, they are not so much concerned with where you are going
As how soon before you come back.

On the night before you leave home for the first time . . .
When you are thinking about a world
That is moving faster than a comet
With opportunities whirling like the stars in a Van Gogh,
Your parents will lie awake, quiet, still,
Lost in their thoughts of how much they love you,
How proud they are of what you are becoming . . .

And before they fall asleep
In the coolness of the sheets and your impending absence,
With full knowledge of all the joys and challenges that await you,
One of them will turn to the other and say,

"Well, she's come this far . . . how did we get so lucky?"

WHEN IS IT TIME
TO LEAVE COACHING?

Assuming you aren't kicked out the door, when is it time to leave the coaching profession? It may depend on what motivated you throughout your career, whether or not you have developed a passion outside the coaching profession, whether or not you have the skills to be successful in another profession, whether you can afford to leave, and for some of us, whether or not we can give up an addiction. Maybe another way to approach the issue is to ask when *should we consider* leaving coaching?

When I retired from coaching volleyball at the University of Nebraska, I was fifty-three years old, at the peek of my professional career, with a supportive administration, and a freshmen class that was one of the best, if not the best, in college volleyball. I had a contract which stated I could not be paid less than the women's basketball coach, who this year will have a salary close to a million dollars a year. *What was I thinking?*

Several factors weighed into my decision to become a mentor to coaches and leave the coaching profession. When I began coaching in the early 1970s, it would take me less than a month to recover from the season. By 2000 I was barely recovering, both physically and mentally, from the stress of the previous season when preseason practice was beginning in August. I was battling diverticulitis on an annual basis that became so acute it required surgery in 2002. One of my closest friends, Paul Hammel, shared the observation when we were fishing recently, that I was a different person during the season. I didn't ask him what he meant, but I'm sure he wasn't referring to being a more balanced human being.

In 1999, I had seen our oldest daughter Katherine play only one collegiate match in her first three years as a setter at Colorado State University because of conflicts with my own team. In her junior year I left the Nebraska team as it changed planes in Denver on a return trip to Lincoln. I tried to rent a car to drive to Fort Collins, Colorado, only to discover my driver's license had expired the day before. I then took a cab from the Denver airport to Moby Gym in Fort Collins in time to get to see her play on a Sunday afternoon before returning on a later flight that evening.

The year before, my long-time assistant Cathy Noth left coaching following our appearance in the NCAA Division I Final Four in Madison, Wisconsin, to pursue a family and other interests. Cathy had been a great fit for me. Her strengths complimented my weaknesses. She had the ability to tell me who had done a great job on the "B" side of the net during practice when I was focused on the core group of players who would see the most playing time. I then could take that information and interact with players I might not have without Cathy's sense of inclusiveness. I did not look forward to the time and energy it would take to develop that level of trust with another head assistant.

The mindset that dominated my coaching career was my competitiveness, or perhaps more precisely, an intense focus of doing everything possible not to lose. It was not so much a celebration in the joy of winning, as wanting to avoid the anguish that came from losing. I should note while this trait may have some value in a competitive environment it does not work so well in parenting or developing a healthy spousal relationship.

There was also what Swiss psychiatrist C.G. Jung refers to as a *shadow side* to my intense competiveness. I had a strong urge to create rather than compete. I found as much pleasure in writing an essay or poem as I did in trying to win a match with Texas or Stanford. By 2000 I was growing tired of trying to beat people. I wanted to exercise different muscles, and different parts of my brain. I wanted to explore the shadow side of my personality and to do that I would have to leave coaching, not because I didn't love the profession, but because coaching didn't allow me the time and opportunity to explore the components of creativity that I had not been able to focus on. I didn't want to wake up when I was seventy-five and realize I hadn't responded to all of my passions.

It was scary. I would be making significantly less money. I would be giving up something I knew I could do well. Perhaps most importantly I would be giving up my identity as the head coach of Nebraska volleyball for something much less public, with fewer external rewards, and with a destination that I couldn't even articulate. During my final season I grieved what I was giving up every night when I went to bed. The following January, I would become a mentor coach for the nineteen sports at Nebraska and help John Cook as he transitioned into the role of head coach. The transition would be smooth because John had developed relationships with the players, and he had a season to reacquaint himself with the culture that surrounds Nebraska volleyball.

It is now twelve years since I have prepared for a season of Nebraska volleyball. I have missed preparing for big matches. I have missed the joy of seeing a player take a risk and work to develop a skill or movement that she didn't have when she arrived. But I miss those things less and less with each year.

When I left coaching, friendships (even those in the volleyball world) transitioned with me. I am in better physical health and I have the time to daydream, read a book, stand in rivers with a fly rod, and on the best days write something worth reading. It is not a better life but a different life, complete with different challenges, rewards, and disappointments.

When people ask me if I miss coaching I sometimes think of the words of one of my own mentors, the poet William Stafford who wrote a poem titled, "On Quitting A Little College." The poem ends with the words:

> *I miss it now*
> *but go*
> *in my own way to my own place.*

TERRY PETTIT

FICTION, COACHING, AND FRIENDSHIP

I have 225 Facebook friends. Approximately thirty are former players whom I have great affection and appreciation for. Fifteen are family members; including a sister-in-law who bakes edible art in the shapes of camels and deciduous trees, and cupcakes so angelic they look as though they are about to levitate. Another ten or so are coaches whom I have had a professional relationship with. That leaves 120 or so whom I would not recognize if they knocked on the door and asked me if I wanted to play Wiffle ball, an activity that in my mind is the sign of a true friend, of which I have six.

Recently I have come to believe that communication falls into two categories: fiction and marketing. Fiction includes poems, love letters, notes on the refrigerator, biographies, postcards on vacation, coffee house conversation, pillow talk, text messages, and memory.

Marketing is everything else: Facebook photos, "fair and balanced" news, press conferences, pregame interviews, postgame interviews, media guides, State of the Union addresses, the Dow Jones Industrial Average, resumés, the pause that a left-handed pitcher makes with a runner on first, talk radio, sermons, graffiti, deep sighs before turning away from your spouse, and pregame speeches before the big match.

The difference between fiction and marketing is intent. Facebook profile pictures are a combination of fiction and marketing, at least for me. My pictures include a 1971 blue Mercedes SL, Ernie Banks, Bob Pettit, Winky Dink, Bugs Bunny, a Herman Leonard jazz photograph (my favorite), a caddy badge from Gary Country Club (now defunct and marketed as New Innsbruck Country Club), and an "Our Gang" type photograph of my brother and I holding jelly sandwiches in 1952. For a week or so an image is my Facebook profile photo. It lets me advertise an implied relationship, mindset, or point of view.

Although I saw him play several games at Wrigley Field, I never met Ernie Banks. I am not related to the former St. Louis Hawk, Bob Pettit, who has the same facial bone structure as my father. I don't own a Mercedes SL. I don't even know who is playing the sax in the Herman Leonard photograph. Winky Dink and Bugs Bunny held my attention on Saturday mornings as a child, and for three summers I was a caddy at Gary Country Club. My brother Jack has posted the picture of us holding sandwiches on his Facebook page as well, although we have chosen different captions (marketing).

With the exception of Anne, Katherine, and Emma, my six closest friends are all males. (Females are not only less likely to play golf; they are completely unwilling to talk about golf after playing golf.) I have known my best friends for at least twenty years and some of them for close to fifty. Most of them I have fished with and ridden for miles on two-laned roads without saying a word. I would best describe our friendship as something like a pick-up baseball game. It is unorganized and comfortable. It can happen at any time. The geography is irrelevant.

What does this have to do with coaching? For some of us coaching is closer to an addiction than a vocation. We daydream about rotations at the dinner table and have nightmares about players who never get it. We become fixated on our program not getting enough attention when we win and getting too much when players transfer or struggle with off-the-court issues. The world that spins around our coaching life seems like a parallel universe which only intrudes when there are big events: the graduation and marriage of a son or daughter, sickness, divorce, or the youngest child leaving for college.

This past summer I turned sixty-seven. I am more than a decade beyond coaching as a vocation and I am beginning to feel that any form of communicating other than spending time with my family and close friends in face-to-face conversation is like playing pinball with flippers that don't work.

In June my best friend and I hiked up to Dream Lake in Rocky Mountain National Park where we fished for greenback cutthroat trout that were feeding on midges at 10,000 feet. There were other people at the lake but everyone else scampered down the mountain when thunderheads sprouted above us like peonies. We stayed and fished for awhile, courting just enough danger to make the journey memorable, then later skirted off the glacier and followed the path down to the parking lot. I was completely exhausted by the time we reached the car, but I knew before I closed the door I had just experienced one of the best days of my life.

I am lucky to have a few friends who worked hard at maintaining a friendship when I was almost entirely focused on winning and losing. To the younger coaches who are chipping away at careers and a legacy, I suggest that you work hard to find ways to develop lifetime conversations and friendships that will become more important than you can imagine. If you do, when the competition in the arena ends, you are likely to have a rich and textured life waiting for you on the path.

A FRESH SEASON:
THE NEBRASKA COLISEUM AND THE
ARCHITECTURE OF COMPETITION

We shape our buildings, and afterwards our buildings shape us.
— Winston Churchill

"It's *time," she said, as she tapped me on the shoulder and ushered me out onto the sidewalk, through swirling cottonwood leaves, away from fans funneling into the Coliseum to watch one of the last collegiate women's volleyball matches that would ever be played in the Nebraska Coliseum. Nebraska was hosting The Ohio State Buckeyes and had invited former Husker players and coaches back for a ceremony following the match.*

She was a television reporter who said she wanted to ask me one question about the building that had been home to Nebraska women's volleyball for the previous thirty-five years; a building that some, including myself, considered the best venue for women's collegiate volleyball in the country, a building that would be no longer host intercollegiate athletics when the volleyball team moved into a twenty-million-dollar renovation at the Bob Devaney Sports Center in the Fall of 2013.

"What moment will you remember most from your years of coaching in the Coliseum?" she asked.

"It's not what you might think it would be," I replied. "Some people would think it would be a particular match, like the win over Penn State in a regional final in 1996 when we were down 11-5 in the fifth set

and won 20-18 to advance to the Final Four. There were other matches as well: A great late-season match with Florida in 1995 when we were the top-two ranked teams in the country. The noise in the Coliseum was so loud that Florida's All-American middle blocker, Aycan Gokberk, caught the ball at a critical point in the fifth set because she thought she heard a referee's whistle. In October of 1985 I remember coming down to the Coliseum two hours before a match with Hawaii and seeing a line of people going out the door, down the block, and around the corner. In 1978 we won our first AIAW Regional Championship in the Coliseum, beating Southwest Missouri for the first time. There were other memorable matches with Texas, Illinois, Penn State, Stanford, UCLA, Pacific, Wisconsin, and Big 8 and Big 12 opponents."

"Those were all special moments, but let me tell you what I will always carry with me. Once or twice a season I would arrive at practice late because of a meeting across campus, and I would walk past my office, out onto the balcony, and take a seat where I could look down on practice taking place below me. From that distance, maybe two hundred feet or so, I would find myself admiring the discipline, the teaching, and the talent on the floor. It reminded me of a great theater troupe preparing for a play. When you are up close, particularly in a match, it is easy to see everything that needs to be fixed, but when I would sit there by myself at that distance, with no coaching agenda, I would lose my breath for a second as I realized I was a part of something special and I got to do it in the Coliseum with these people every day."

I first entered the Nebraska Coliseum in the summer of 1977, when I came to Lincoln to interview for the head coaching position for Nebraska women's volleyball. Dr. June B. Davis, the senior women's administrator, asked me as part of the interview to run a brief practice with six players who were in Lincoln for the summer. I thought it was a brilliant idea for several reasons: it would give the Nebraska athletic administration the opportunity to watch me coach, it would give me the chance to evaluate some of the returning players, and it would help me see if I had the coaching skills to improve the talent that was already there.

For forty-five minutes, I had the players work in groups of two, executing ball handling drills in a confined area, passing to themselves, setting to themselves, drop-stepping and passing to their partners. After the short practice I had the chance to ask the players a few questions. There was a general theme to their questions of wanting to have more demanded of them. They seemed earnest about wanting to get better. Nancy Grant, a sophomore outside hitter said, "We play well during the season but we tend to fall off as we approach the regional tournament. We need to be pushed."

I thought I was pretty good at *pushing people* so I accepted the job offer three days later after Nebraska's first choice turned the job down. The decision would impact our family in several ways. We would move from a small town in the Piedmont of North Carolina where I had been an associate professor of English at a junior college, as well the women's volleyball, men's golf, and men's tennis coach. My wife would be leaving a junior high teaching position in math and looking for a new teaching job in Lincoln. It meant that in my immediate future I would be giving up the role I had prepared for as a college creative writing teacher to become a full time coach. It also meant that for the next twenty-three years I would spend more time in the Nebraska Coliseum than any other combination of buildings that I have lived or worked in.

The Nebraska Coliseum, built in 1926, was host to several major events during its first fifty years, from concerts and plays, to graduation ceremonies, and the boys' state basketball championship finals. The Coliseum was large enough to host seven state championship games at one time in the 1930s, but when the athletic department departed the building in November of 1976 for the Bob Devaney Sports Center, named after the legendary football coach and current athletic director, the Coliseum was left with only one custodian for the main floor and no maintenance personnel. The brown and ochre colored playing court hid several dead spots where a basketball didn't return to the fingertips of the dribbler. Most of the windows in the balcony were cracked or broken. Faded red curtains separated the main court from a colonnade of arches that surrounded the playing floor. The hooks holding the curtains were arthritic or gone, and when I pulled the curtains into place for practice some of the fabric disintegrated with each tug. Sunlight streamed through the broken windows above the balcony and made it difficult for volleyball players to pass the ball.

Despite the disrepair on the inside, there was still evidence that important events had once taken place in a building that had hosted Elvis Presley, Bob Hope, Wilt Chamberlain, and President Richard Nixon. In addition to that, almost every male in the state over thirty years old had played or watched a state championship basketball game in the Coliseum.

A large Longines clock, the same type of clock that was in Yankee Stadium, hung on the south wall, keeping accurate time twice a day. Two enormous four-sided FairPlay scoreboards hung like udders from arched rafters that ran the width of the Coliseum playing floor. Beneath one of the scoreboards the greatest basketball game in Nebraska basketball history took place in 1958 when James Kubacki, who had spent the first three quarters in street clothes seated on the bench because of a knee injury, begged Nebraska head coach Jerry Bush to allow him to suit up and enter play when team captain Gary Reimers left the game with leg cramps.

The Cornhuskers were playing Kansas who had beaten Nebraska 102-46 just two weeks earlier in Lawrence, and featured seven foot center Wilt Chamberlain who was averaging thirty points a game and had rendered the term "matchup" obsolete. In a scenario that would rival the movie *Hoosiers*, Kubacki entered the game with two minutes and forty-seven seconds left and sank a jump shot with twenty-seven seconds on the clock as the Cornhuskers upset the Jayhawks, 43-41. Nebraska basketball fans have warmed themselves over that victory for fifty-five years while waiting for the men's basketball program to win its first NCAA tournament game.

In 1956 Elvis Presley, wearing a yellow sports coat with black stripes and a blue iridescent shirt with kimono collar, played the Coliseum to 3,000 screaming fans. A good friend of mine, Dave Higgins, was sitting on the back steps, disappointed that he didn't have a ticket to the show and hoping to sneak in if he had the opportunity, when the doors opened and Presley stepped out to have a cigarette. Higgins was so surprised he couldn't speak, but Presley correctly assessed the situation and gave Higgins two tickets to the front row.

Bob Hope and President Richard Nixon visited the Coliseum in 1971, one to take peoples' minds off the war in Vietnam and the President because Nebraska, a state known for both conservative thought and courteous behavior, was one of the few college campuses Nixon thought he could give a public speech without engaging derisive interference especially if he spent time congratulating Nebraska's number one ranked football team. (Nixon's speech did elicit some protests from both campus and non-campus groups.)

Sometimes I would take potential recruits to the Nebraska State Capitol, located a few blocks from the campus, where we would take the elevator up to the observation deck on the fifteenth floor just under the statue of *The Sower* that stands atop the dome. At street level *The Sower* looks somewhat like a volleyball player hitting a cut shot, at least that is what I told recruits. From the observation deck, the Coliseum sits to the north in the middle of campus. With ten Roman columns in front and an arched roof covering a brick building that could house a Boeing 747, the Coliseum grips the earth with a countenance that is almost Egyptian.

If an F3 tornado blew into Lincoln from the southwest, one could imagine most of the downtown, including the restaurants in the Haymarket, the banks on 13th Street and the bars on "O" Street, would be swept up into a cloud of limestone and steel that wouldn't stop before it reached the Platte River thirty-five miles to the east. The only thing left standing in the debris field would be the Coliseum, Sphinx-like, as it looked out over the salt flat that once was downtown Lincoln.

There was no indication these trips to the top of the Nebraska State Capitol ever impacted a recruit one way or the other, but the view of Coliseum and the surrounding countryside never failed to impress me.

In the beginning it took a pair of work gloves, a pair of Vise-Grips, a good supply of C-clamps, eyebolts, turn buckles, and an hour and a half to set up the six volleyball standards and five nets that were anchored into a balcony at one end and the stage at the other. In 1977, if we set up one net we had to set up them all. The standards were made of heavy steel with a large rectangular base that sometimes screwed into a floor plate. Replacement parts were hard to come by because the gymnastics company that made the standards was growing broke from lawsuits.

For competitions, players set up two rows of wooden chairs on the sidelines, which initially were all we needed to seat parents and a few friends. For the first match against Drake University on September 10, 1977, my wife brought an aluminum pan to cook hot dogs in for the concession stand and a cooler for lemonade. Barbara was six months pregnant with our daughter Katherine who would grow up hitting volleyballs against the wall in the concourse during practice, pretending if she didn't hit ten in a row, without the ball bounding down the hall, she wouldn't play in college.

The match took place beneath lighting more appropriate for a thrift shop. On the stage beneath the proscenium arch to the north, karate students advanced and retreated throughout the day and into the night, oblivious to the volleyball competition at the south end of the arena. Because there was no way to secure the playing floor for practice, the team manager spent most of her time shepherding basketball players, baton twirlers, jugglers, and occasionally homeless people who came into the Coliseum for warmth, onto the concourse where faculty and students were continually circling the main floor, jogging thirteen laps to the mile.

The atmosphere inside the Coliseum teetered on a line between quaint and unfortunate. It was hard to foresee within a dozen years the Nebraska Coliseum would again become a vibrant and beloved venue for the University of Nebraska Athletic Department. But athletic venues only become beloved if the home team wins consistently over a significant period of time. The only exception I think of to this rule is Wrigley Field, the home of the Chicago Cubs. Wrigley Field is an outdoor restaurant where tourists who don't keep score on scorecards eat Chicago style hot dogs and drink $8 beers through the seventh inning, while looking out over a beautifully manicured lawn to yachts cruising above the grandstands on Lake Michigan. It is like a scene out of the movie *The Truman Show*. No one expects the Cubs to win.

The Boston Garden, without the seventeen NBA championship banners that hang from the rafters, is a dark and dingy arena with a funny floor. If tournament golf hadn't been invented at the Old Course at St. Andrews, and if it were not a part of the British Open's regular rotation, it would just be a pasture suitable for Scottish Blackface sheep. There are many things that make the Coliseum a special venue, but the most impressive thing about the building is from September 2, 1976 through December 15, 2012, Nebraska women's volleyball won 524 matches while losing only thirty-four matches, for a winning percentage of .967.

The primary reason for that level of success can be attributed to exceptional talent (the majority of the players were Nebraskans or from nearby states), committed to working very hard at becoming extraordinary volleyball players with the help of strong coaching and administrative support. But to a person, players and coaches speak with great affection about the Coliseum playing a significant role in developing a culture that led to Nebraska volleyball's remarkable success.

The original Coliseum in Rome, where gladiators had epic competitions, hunts, plays, and sea battles was completed in 80 A.D. The word *arena* comes from the Roman word for sand and refers to the floor of the Roman Coliseum that soaked up the blood from these battles. The Nebraska Coliseum with its proscenium arch above the stage, the arches that separate the concourses from the volleyball court, its arched roof, and the Roman columns that fans pass through when entering the building, evokes the Coliseum in Rome and implies that *something important is happening here*. It does not feel like a modern multi-purpose building that might host a basketball game tonight, a convention for actuaries tomorrow, and a model railroad swap meet on the weekend. Because it reminds us of the great architecture of the Coliseum in Rome, because of the intimacy of 4,000 spectators surrounding the court, and because of the many details that a fan might not even be consciously aware of, the Nebraska Coliseum creates an atmosphere where both competitors and spectators become emotionally engaged and enter the competition with high expectations.

This was certainly not true when I coached my first match in the Coliseum in the fall of 1977, when the Huskers hosted Drake University with less than 100 fans in attendance. Gradually, beginning with small improvements and consistent success on the court, which led to more administrative support including a major renovation in 1990, the Coliseum came to be the best volleyball venue in the country for close to twenty-five years.

While most contemporary American architecture is designed to be spectacular and attract attention on the outside, the Nebraska Coliseum is designed in a way for the people on the inside of the building to feel important. This is not an easy thing to do, and the reason for it is that the Coliseum was designed with a sense of human proportion, much of it stemming from the golden ratio (sometimes referred to as the golden mean, golden rule or golden rectangle), which has inspired mathematicians, biologists, architects, and artists for at least 2,400 years.

The golden ratio occurs in nature in the spirals of a nautilus shell, the eye of a daisy, the proportions of the human face and even in the "lub dub" of our heartbeat. The ratio is approximately 1.618, is very pleasing to the eye, and is a major component of classic design.

Elements of architecture that are not in proportion leave us uncomfortable. Think of a person who has an unusually long and narrow face, or a small house that is built with an unusually high entrance, a large room with a very low ceiling or perhaps you can remember the Pontiac Aztec, one of the worst looking cars ever designed. (For more information on the golden ratio and other patterns in timeless architecture you could read Christopher Alexander's book, *A Pattern Language*.)

The golden ratio occurs hundreds of times in the Nebraska Coliseum in the shape of a very pleasing rectangle. It first makes its appearance in the rectangle formed by the ten Roman columns as you enter the building. Each of the arches that line the concourses is in the shape of the golden rectangle. The trophy cases built into the arches in the foyer of the Coliseum and the banners hanging from the rafters mimic the golden rectangle. There is a very large golden rectangle formed by the playing court in relationship to the height of the lighting above the court. Each letter that forms the word NEBRASKA behind the end lines of the court is another example of the golden rectangle.

Players and spectators are not consciously aware of this deliberate sense of design when a match is being played, but unconsciously everyone *feels* the impact of being in a space where everything is in proportion. Everyone is comfortable because so many elements in the design of the Coliseum are integrated with a mathematical ratio that occurs in Leonardo's *Mona Lisa*, in the spiral shape of the pineapple they may have eaten for breakfast, and in the geometry of a volleyball set from the setter from her position at the net to an outside hitter on the final play of the match.

While the Nebraska Coliseum has always had the bones that make up great architecture there were several refinements made through the years that made it a better venue for both volleyball players and spectators. One of the most important decisions was when we decided not to play matches in the same direction as the original basketball competition court.

The Coliseum basketball court was ninety-four feet long and fifty feet wide with a large amount of space at each end. A regulation volleyball court is only sixty feet long and thirty feet wide, which would have created an enormous amount of empty space beyond the end lines. Locating the volleyball court on the south end of the Coliseum floor and running it perpendicular to the original basketball court created a much more intimate atmosphere and allowed people to sit in the balconies close to the action on three sides. One of the problems with contemporary venues is that a majority of the spectators are too far from the action. The volleyball court, which fits snugly into the south end of the Coliseum, created an arena where spectators feel like they are participants.

The ten columns on the front of the Coliseum form a golden rectangle, as do the Coliseum court and its NCAA National Championship banners hanging above.

A major renovation took place in the Coliseum following the 1990 season which included a new playing floor, scoreboards designed to fit on the balcony façade, a new sound system, restrooms, concession stands, and lighting, while doubling the bleacher seating on the sideline that did not have a balcony. The coaching offices were moved from the former custodial closet off the main court to a huddle of small offices on the second floor just off the balcony. The locker rooms were renovated and a ready room was created next to the locker room for players to meet with the coaching staff before competition. The lighting above the court was tripled and was directed onto the players without making it difficult for the setter to pick up the ball on a high pass or dig. The goal was to the light the Coliseum court as if it were a Broadway stage. With the renovation, attendance increased from an average of 1,800 in the later 1980s to over 3,500 with some crowds approaching 4,500 depending upon the alertness of the fire marshal.

The renovation came very close to not happening. In the mid-1980s the campus was in desperate need for indoor recreational facilities. At the time the Coliseum was the primary recreation center for students and the main floor was in use anytime the volleyball team was not practicing or playing. It was not unusual in the early years to have pickup basketball games happening sixty feet away from practice.

The University planned to solve the problem by building a new recreation facility that would be connected to the Coliseum and either raise the volleyball court to the balcony level, which would provide more space for potential Health, Physical Education, and Recreation (HPER) offices, or move the volleyball court into the new recreation center, which would limit seating to 1,800 people, an attendance figure we had surpassed for several years.

Moving the volleyball court to the balcony level would have destroyed both the beauty and the sense of proportion that was instrumental to the design of the Coliseum. The playing space would have felt like a Quonset hut that seated 2,000 people. This was the plan that the University was advocating because it was the least expensive option. The athletic department, with the exceptions of Dr. Barbara Hibner, the senior women's administrator, and the volleyball staff, didn't fully realize the level of community support the program had cultivated nor the revenue potential for a venue that would seat more than 4,000 spectators.

At my urging we began selling season tickets for volleyball in 1987. No one else in the athletic department believed it would help attendance or create significant revenues. (During my last year as head coach in 1999, The Match Club, the volleyball team's booster club, sold more than $200,000 in t-shirts and the Coliseum was beginning to sell out which has continued throughout John Cook's coaching tenure.)

My most important supporter in fighting the University's plan was Dr. Hibner, who led by persuading our former football coach and current athletic director, Bob Devaney, to join with us in opposing the initial plan. Over time, both the HPER department and the Campus Recreation department joined us in proposing a third option because there would be challenges for them as well if volleyball left the Coliseum or stayed and moved up to the balcony level. HPER faculty didn't want to hear the screeching of shoes and thump of balls through the ceilings of their new offices, and Campus Recreation wasn't keen on volleyball becoming a primary tenant in their new facility. Sometimes fear can be a great ally.

The revised plan seemed to please everyone. HPER would remain in Mabel Lee Hall, but would have more space and not be distracted by the noise of competition. Campus Recreation would get a new facility it would not have to share with the athletic department. Nebraska volleyball would stay in the Coliseum and receive some of the elements that would allow it to promote and grow the sport to a greater level than many believed possible.

The renovation would take a year to complete. For this plan to work Nebraska volleyball would have to play its 1991 competitive season in the Bob Devaney Sports Center, home to Nebraska men's and women's basketball. Danny Nee, the men's basketball head coach was not eager to have volleyball floor plates installed on his court. Coach Nee was not unique in his thinking among NCAA Division I men's basketball coaches, but Nebraska volleyball was averaging more than 2,000 fans a match in 1989 and to play a season in a high school facility would have done irreparable harm to the program. The only person who could resolve this issue was Coach Devaney, who was beginning to experience the first signs of memory loss and had both good days and bad days with regards to his ability to organize his thoughts and make decisions that affected the department.

In June of 1991, I called Coach Devaney's office and asked Jan Eby, his long-time secretary, if it would be a good day to take Coach Devaney over to talk with Coach Nee about the floor plates. Jan thought it was, but she couldn't guarantee how long Coach Devaney's current mindset would last. I drove over to South Stadium and went into Coach Devaney's office where I reminded him of the need to play our matches in the Devaney Center because of construction in the Coliseum. Coach

Devaney listened, nodded his head but he didn't say anything.

On the way over to Coach Nee's office, Coach Devaney said several things that didn't make any sense to me. Some of it had to do with boxing, some of it with football, some of it wasn't in complete sentences. He seemed disoriented and I was concerned that he wouldn't be able to make my case to Coach Nee. We parked the car in the lot behind the Devaney Center and walked into the basketball suite where Coach Nee was standing by his desk. Without hesitation and in a clear and decisive voice Coach Devaney said, "Danny, there is construction in the Coliseum this fall, so Terry will need to play his matches in the Devaney Center and we will need to put in floor plates as soon as possible." He had willed himself into being up to the task at hand. Coach Nee, said that he "understood and there would be no problem." On the way back to South Stadium, Coach Devaney returned to a conversation that only he understood.

I had great affection for Coach Devaney, as did almost everyone who ever worked for him. He was a very competitive person, which certainly helped the development of women's athletics in its beginning stages. He had great timing and a great sense of humor. He was very direct in his communication and you always knew where you stood with him. To my knowledge he only came to one volleyball match. The senior women's administrator brought him to a match in 1978. He thought we won the match when we won the second game and came out on the court to shake my hand and congratulate me. I didn't want to embarrass him by telling him that we had at least one more game to play, so we shook hands and he went on his way with Dr. Davis. The opposing coach looked over at me from his huddle with a somewhat bewildered look, so I just smiled and shrugged my shoulders.

The renovation set the stage for the next twenty-three years of tremendous success, including Nebraska's first NCAA National Championship in 1995. Under John Cook, Nebraska earned a second national title in his first year as head coach in 2000, and followed it up with another in 2006.

In essence, we had created a theater for volleyball. A large portion of the matches were being produced by Nebraska Educational Television (NETV), which under the leadership of Rod Bates, went to great pains to discover the best camera angles and provide what I believe was the best televised production of volleyball in the country. The Match Club raised money to provide renovations to the locker rooms and later helped to fund foreign trips. Success and television coverage made the Coliseum the place to be and the place to be seen.

A thirty-piece band was part of the matches from the early 1980s and helped to create an electric atmosphere while season tickets to women's volleyball became as cherished as those to football. (Coach Cook told me that individual tickets to the 2012 Texas match in the Coliseum were being sold on the street for $400 each.)

All of these changes only created a more intimate environment for the players. Every Nebraska volleyball player I have ever seen interviewed, when asked what she appreciated most about her playing volleyball for Nebraska has said the same thing: the fans' support and playing in the Coliseum.

When I asked several players who had competed or coached in the Coliseum from the mid-1980s through the last match in 2012 about their strongest memories of playing in the Coliseum, there were several consistent themes:

They loved how it felt as if the fans were almost on top of them.

They could remember times when the noise level was so high they could feel the floor shaking beneath them.

They loved having their name announced over the public address system and the response from fans.

They loved playing on the Coliseum floor, which was easy on their feet when they jumped and landed. (It was engineered with hard maple laid over rubber balls on top of plywood.)

They loved the stomping of feet, the clapping of hands, and the deafening roar that would accompany a point when the team was in danger.

They loved the smell of the popcorn that permeated the building from the concession stands.

They loved interacting with fans after matches, signing autographs, and having their pictures taken with young kids holding miniature volleyballs.

They recalled when they were tired and not playing well, that the energy in the building was like an influx of oxygen allowing them to come back and compete.

They loved how the noise could impact an opponent in the end of a set.

They loved how there was a sense of importance to what they did.

Karen Dahlgren, a walk-on from Bertrand, Nebraska, who led her team to the NCAA National Championship match and was named 1986 National Player of the Year, and who later became head women's volleyball coach at the University of Kansas, remembered:

"One of my most vivid memories of the Coliseum was as an opposing coach during my first year as an assistant at Kansas. We were traveling by the small bus that KU owned, which had given us some trouble on our very first trip earlier that year to Wichita State. The bus broke down in St. Joseph, Missouri, and we had to call for a charter bus to continue to Lincoln. Since we had to wait for some time for the bus to arrive, we were quite late getting to Lincoln for the match — in fact I think we arrived at the time the match was scheduled to begin. The players changed and got taped on the bus because we knew we would go straight to the court and our warm-up time would begin immediately. Normally the gyms that volleyball matches are played in fill with spectators as warm-ups are taking place,

so none of us were prepared for the site of the Coliseum being full and the cheers from the crowd when we walked onto the court. The entire crowd gave us a rousing ovation for making it to the match. It was both welcoming and intimidating at the same time."

Fiona Nepo, a three time All-American setter from Honolulu, who played from 1995-99, recalled a match that to many Nebraska fans is the epitome of what the Coliseum is all about:

"I remember my first time in the Coliseum, during my recruiting trip, when I was sitting with Stephanie Thater munching on some popcorn and I was amazed at the atmosphere as the Huskers ran onto the court. In that moment I made my decision to play for Nebraska. There was a picture of Lori Endicott hanging in the volleyball office on the second floor of the Coliseum and every day I walked into the office to watch film or meet with the coaches, I always glanced at that picture of Lori because she was my motivation to carry on the 'Great Setters' tradition at Nebraska.

"There are many matches I can recall, but the one that stays with me the most has to be the match we played against Penn State in the 1996 NCAA Regional Finals. I remember walking into the locker room, donning my uniform, heading to the trainers to get taped, and then getting ready for our pregame meeting. As we waited to go up to the courts, by the bottom of the stairs I was giddy like always before a game. I ran up those stairs and smelled the popcorn while running through the fans who were waiting to get in or find a seat and then there was the best feeling when you broke through the red curtains and stepped onto the playing court with the band playing, the crowd cheering and singing, 'There is no place like Nebraska.' It was an indescribable feeling.

"Being announced by Steve Johnson was always the best feeling before the game because after he would announce my name, the Coliseum would respond with a 'Feeeeeeee'. I loved it! I remember that we were down 11-5 in the fifth set and I kept getting tooled on the right side. I remember the crowd cheering and me grimacing when I would get tooled. I believe I set Megan Korver the last three points and we won 20-18! The Coliseum went crazy and so did we as we piled to the floor!"

Korver, an All-American middle who had just transferred back to Nebraska also recalled the match with Penn State:

"It was my first year at Nebraska after transferring home from George Washington. I stepped in as starter at middle blocker because a preseason injury took Jen McFadden out of the lineup. Penn State has always been a rival of Nebraska and it was a very intense match. We were in the fifth set, behind 11-5 when we started to come back and tie it up and then we went ahead by one point. The place was rocking and when it appeared that we won the next point to win the match both Kate Crnich and Coach Pettit jumped into the air, but the officials called it back and we had to regroup.

"It got quiet . . . but then I remember Fiona called my number and set a slide that I hit for a kill. The fans were so loud the floor shook and I couldn't hear what Fiona was saying but I saw her body language and hand gestures and I understood she would be coming back to me in transition if we got the opportunity, and we did. She set me another slide and the place exploded.

"The win against Penn State set the team up for a return trip to the NCAA Final Four, but that play set me up for the next two years at Nebraska. Not only did my confidence increase, but also my relationship with Fiona and the other players changed and was on a different level. Looking back, I think it was my

first step into leadership and it had a tremendous impact into the self-confidence that I have today."

Every player who was contacted on that team had a very similar response regarding the importance of the 1996 NCAA Regional Championship match, even though many of them had played on a NCAA National Championship team the year before. I don't think there is a more transformational event for an athlete than to come back when it appears that you have lost to a great opponent.

The match impacted more than just the players. John Cook, the Wisconsin head coach, watched the match from the balcony. His Badgers had lost in the semifinals to the Huskers the night before. After the match John said that it was the best volleyball match he had ever seen. I have no doubt that the atmosphere in the Coliseum that night had some influence on John's decision to leave the formidable program he was building in Madison and come back to Nebraska to be the head coach in 2000.

The Nebraska Athletic Director, Bill Byrne, who had followed Coach Devaney in 1993, was sitting with a Fiesta Bowl representative several rows behind the Nebraska bench. After the press conference, Bill told me the Fiesta Bowl representative told him that the match was the best athletic event he had ever seen. Bill agreed.

In my own mind, the level of athlete or the level of play might have been replicated elsewhere in collegiate women's volleyball, but the staging of the event in the Nebraska Coliseum not only took the match to a completely different level, it also allowed a team that returned only two starters from a team that had lost four All-Americans (three to graduation and one to injury) to advance the NCAA Final Four against a very talented and well-coached Penn State squad.

I thought about some of these things as I watched the last volleyball match I would ever see in the Coliseum last October. The former coaches and players who had been invited back were introduced after the match and each received a medallion designed by George

Lundeen, the world-class sculptor who had designed *The Players*, the bronze that was installed in the Coliseum entrance in 1991 as part of the renovation. The sculpture depicts three women risking everything to be a part of the game and was paid for before it was installed by selling a limited edition of smaller replicas to collectors and Nebraska volleyball enthusiasts.

After the match, seventy former players, many of them in tears, walked across the court in front of the bench of the current Nebraska team that had just lost a tough match to Ohio State, and who had only seen many of the alumni in photographs in the Coliseum concourse or heard stories about their achievements. Each of the former players was given a medallion and framed season tickets that depicted the history of Nebraska Volleyball and the Coliseum while receiving congratulations from Coach Cook and myself before they proceeded to have their picture taken with Tom Osborne, the legendary former Nebraska football coach, who was performing one of his last acts as the Director of Nebraska Athletics before retiring at the end of the year.

From where I stood, I could hear comments from the current players seated to my left as they recognized names or whispered something regarding the remarkable fitness and posture of the former players, some of whom had competed decades before them. Then, after the official ceremony, a spontaneous thing happened. The current Huskers left their bench and two lines formed as the current players and the former players passed each other, shaking hands and embracing while they moved in opposite directions, until they became a circle inside a circle and began to merge seamlessly into one large nautilus shell that curled in upon itself in a completely unorganized but natural pattern, all of this happening beneath the shadow of the proscenium arch, and then when the dance was complete, without any hesitation, they shouted in unison the litany that each of them had said when they broke a huddle in the midst of competition for the past forty years:

"We are Nebraska, we are one!"

ABOUT THE AUTHOR

On September 6, 2013 the University of Nebraska named its playing court "Terry Pettit Court" at the state-of-the-art volleyball arena in the Bob Devaney Sports Center in Lincoln, Nebraska. The evening was even more special because Terry and Anne's daughter, Emma, was competing on the court as a setter for the Villanova Wildcats.

For twenty-three years Coach Pettit led one of the most successful NCAA athletic programs in history. During his tenure as head coach, the University of Nebraska women's volleyball team won twenty-one conference championships while leading the nation in All-America and Academic All-America selections. His teams were ranked in the top 10 for the final sixteen years and advanced to the NCAA Championship Finals on six occasions, winning Nebraska's first national championship in volleyball in 1995. He received National Coach of the Year honors in 1986, 1994, and 1996 and was selected to the American Volleyball Coaches Association Hall of Fame in 2009.

Since 2005 Terry Pettit has been mentoring coaches, athletic administrators, and corporations throughout the country. Graduating with a B.S. in English from Manchester University and an M.F.A. in poetry from the Creative Writing Workshop at the University of Arkansas, giving him a unique perspective as a poet, educator, coach, and parent on teambuilding, leadership, and coaching. Terry lives with his wife, Anne, in Fort Collins, Colorado.

A FRESH SEASON

Insights into Coaching,
Leadership, and Volleyball

TERRY PETTIT
NCAA Championship Coach
Mentor to Extraordinary Coaches and Leaders

To order copies of this book or other books
and videos by Terry Pettit, go online to:
www.terrypettit.com.
If you would like Terry Pettit to present
to your organization, please contact him at:
tpettit@terrypettit.com